"After utilizing toolkits from The Art of Service, I was able to identify threats within my organization to which I was completely unaware. Using my team's knowledge as a competitive advantage, we now have superior systems that save time and energy."

"As a new Chief Technology Officer, I was feeling unprepared and inadequate to be successful in my role. I ordered an IT toolkit Sunday night and was prepared Monday morning to shed light on areas of improvement within my organization. I no longer felt overwhelmed and intimidated, I was excited to share what I had learned."

"I used the questionnaires to interview members of my team. I never knew how many insights we could produce collectively with our internal knowledge."

"I usually work until at least 8pm on weeknights. The Art of Service questionnaire saved me so much time and worry that Thursday night I attended my son's soccer game without sacrificing my professional obligations."

"After purchasing The Art of Service toolkit, I was able to identify areas where my company was not in compliance that could have put my job at risk. I looked like a hero when I proactively educated my team on the risks and presented a solid solution."

"I spent months shopping for an external consultant before realizing that The Art of Service would allow my team to consult themselves! Not only did we save time not catching a consultant up to speed, we were able to keep our company information and industry secrets confidential."

"Everyday there are new regulations and processes in my industry. The Art of Service toolkit has kept me ahead by using AI technology to constantly update the toolkits and address emerging needs."

"I customized The Art of Service toolkit to focus specifically on the concerns of my role and industry. I didn't have to waste time with a generic self-help book that wasn't tailored to my exact situation."

"Many of our competitors have asked us about our secret sauce. When I tell them it's the knowledge we have in-house, they never believe me. Little do they know The Art of Service toolkits are working behind the scenes."

"One of my friends hired a consultant who used the knowledge gained working with his company to advise their competitor. Talk about a competitive disadvantage! The Art of Service allowed us to keep our knowledge from walking out the door along with a huge portion of our budget in consulting fees."

"Honestly, I didn't know what I didn't know. Before purchasing The Art of Service, I didn't realize how many areas of my business needed to be refreshed and improved. I am so relieved The Art of Service was there to highlight our blind spots."

"Before The Art of Service, I waited eagerly for consulting company reports to come out each month. These reports kept us up to speed but provided little value because they put our competitors on the same playing field. With The Art of Service, we have uncovered unique insights to drive our business forward."

"Instead of investing extensive resources into an external consultant, we can spend more of our budget towards pursuing our company goals and objectives...while also spending a little more on corporate holiday parties."

"The risk of our competitors getting ahead has been mitigated because The Art of Service has provided us with a 360-degree view of threats within our organization before they even arise."

Secure coding
Complete Self-Assessment Guide

https://theartofservice.com
support@theartofservice.com

Table of Contents

About The Art of Service

The Art of Service, Business Process Architects since 2000, is dedicated to helping stakeholders achieve excellence.

Defining, designing, creating, and implementing a process to solve a stakeholders challenge or meet an objective is the most valuable role… In EVERY group, company, organization and department.

Unless you're talking a one-time, single-use project, there should be a process. Whether that process is managed and implemented by humans, AI, or a combination of the two, it needs to be designed by someone with a complex enough perspective to ask the right questions.

Someone capable of asking the right questions and step back and say, 'What are we really trying to accomplish here? And is there a different way to look at it?'

With The Art of Service's Self-Assessments, we empower people who can do just that — whether their title is marketer, entrepreneur, manager, salesperson, consultant, Business Process Manager, executive assistant, IT Manager, CIO etc... —they are the people who rule the future. They are people who watch the process as it happens, and ask the right questions to make the process work better.

Contact us when you need any support with this Self-Assessment and any help with templates, blue-prints and examples of standard documents you might need:

https://theartofservice.com
support@theartofservice.com

Included Resources - how to access

Included with your purchase of the book is the Secure coding

Self-Assessment Spreadsheet Dashboard which contains all questions and Self-Assessment areas and auto-generates insights, graphs, and project RACI planning - all with examples to get you started right away.

How? Simply send an email to
access@theartofservice.com
with this books' title in the subject to get the Secure coding Self Assessment Tool right away.

The auto reply will guide you further, you will then receive the following contents with New and Updated specific criteria:

- The latest quick edition of the book in PDF
- The latest complete edition of the book in PDF, which criteria correspond to the criteria in...
- The Self-Assessment Excel Dashboard, and...
- Example pre-filled Self-Assessment Excel Dashboard to get familiar with results generation
- In-depth specific Checklists covering the topic
- Project management checklists and templates to assist with implementation

INCLUDES LIFETIME SELF ASSESSMENT UPDATES

Every self assessment comes with Lifetime Updates and Lifetime Free Updated Books. Lifetime Updates is an industry-first feature which allows you to receive verified self assessment updates, ensuring you always have the most accurate information at your fingertips.

Get it now- you will be glad you did - do it now, before you forget.

Send an email to **access@theartofservice.com** with this books' title in the subject to get the Secure coding Self Assessment Tool right away.

Purpose of this Self-Assessment

This Self-Assessment has been developed to improve understanding of the requirements and elements of Secure coding, based on best practices and standards in business process architecture, design and quality management.

It is designed to allow for a rapid Self-Assessment to determine how closely existing management practices and procedures correspond to the elements of the Self-Assessment.

The criteria of requirements and elements of Secure coding have been rephrased in the format of a Self-Assessment questionnaire, with a seven-criterion scoring system, as explained in this document.

In this format, even with limited background knowledge of Secure coding, a manager can quickly review existing operations to determine how they measure up to the standards. This in turn can serve as the starting point of a 'gap analysis' to identify management tools or system elements that might usefully be implemented in the organization to help improve overall performance.

How to use the Self-Assessment

On the following pages are a series of questions to identify to what extent your Secure coding initiative is complete in comparison to the requirements set in standards.

To facilitate answering the questions, there is a space in front of each question to enter a score on a scale of '1' to '5'.

1 Strongly Disagree

2 Disagree

3 Neutral

4 Agree

5 Strongly Agree

Read the question and rate it with the following in front of mind:

**'In my belief,
the answer to this question is clearly defined'.**

There are two ways in which you can choose to interpret this statement;

1. how aware are you that the answer to the question is clearly defined
2. for more in-depth analysis you can choose to gather evidence and confirm the answer to the question. This obviously will take more time, most Self-Assessment users opt for the first way to interpret the question and dig deeper later on based on the outcome of the overall Self-Assessment.

A score of '1' would mean that the answer is not clear at all, where a '5' would mean the answer is crystal clear and defined. Leave emtpy when the question is not applicable or you don't want to answer it, you can skip it without affecting your score. Write your score in the space provided.

After you have responded to all the appropriate statements in each section, compute your average score for that section, using the formula provided, and round to the nearest tenth. Then transfer to the corresponding spoke in the Secure coding Scorecard on the second next page of the Self-Assessment.

Your completed Secure coding Scorecard will give you a clear presentation of which Secure coding areas need attention.

Secure coding Scorecard Example

Example of how the finalized Scorecard can look like:

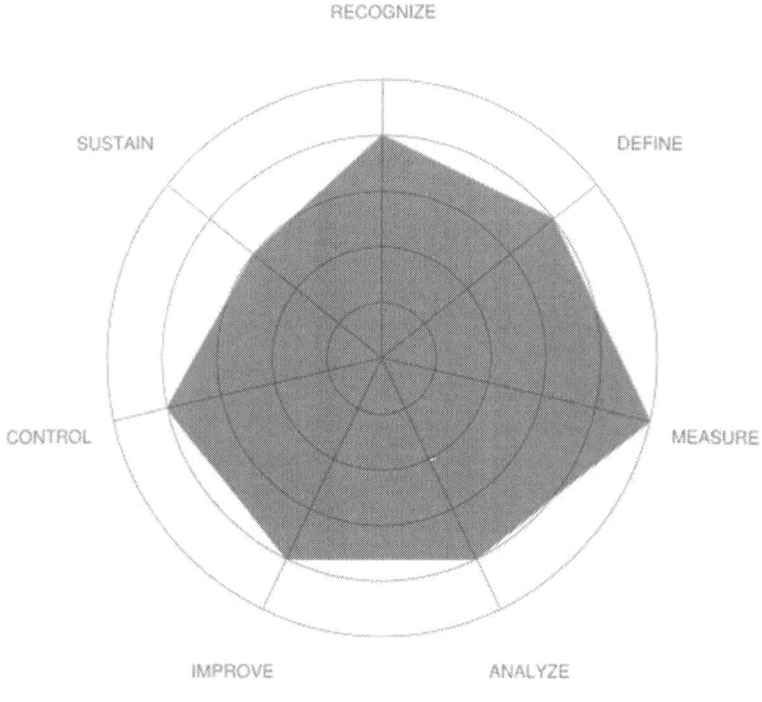

Secure coding Scorecard

Your Scores:

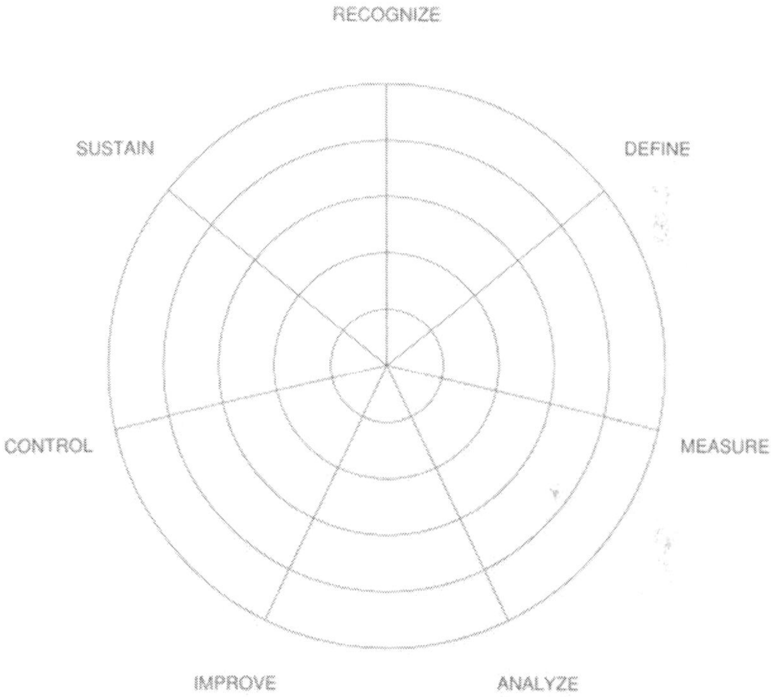

BEGINNING OF THE SELF-ASSESSMENT:

CRITERION #1: RECOGNIZE

INTENT: Be aware of the need for change. Recognize that there is an unfavorable variation, problem or symptom.

In my belief, the answer to this question is clearly defined:

5 Strongly Agree

4 Agree

3 Neutral

2 Disagree

1 Strongly Disagree

1. What new tools or resources does your organization need?
<--- Score

2. What are the expected benefits of Secure coding to the stakeholder?
<--- Score

3. Who else hopes to benefit from it?

<--- Score

4. What information was needed sooner?
<--- Score

5. How should session management vulnerabilities be prevented?
<--- Score

6. What controls are needed to properly secure the environment?
<--- Score

7. Are attacks that target the virtual infrastructure prevented with technical controls?
<--- Score

8. Is there a large clump of issues around a particular module or a particular feature?
<--- Score

9. How big is the security problem?
<--- Score

10. What is your approach to reducing the number of escalated issues and resolving at lowest level possible?
<--- Score

11. What would happen if Secure coding weren't done?
<--- Score

12. What is the minimum amount of information needed to create a resource description in your catalog?

<--- Score

13. What problems are you facing and how do you consider Secure coding will circumvent those obstacles?
<--- Score

14. Are new security features needed or is it necessary to modify existing features?
<--- Score

15. What needs to be done so that cybersecurity is built in to digital goods and services?
<--- Score

16. When can customers obtain an updated version that fixes the issue?
<--- Score

17. What are the stakeholder objectives to be achieved with Secure coding?
<--- Score

18. How will you assess the severity of the identified vulnerabilities?
<--- Score

19. Can an attacker prevent authorized users from accessing the system?
<--- Score

20. As a sponsor, customer or management, how important is it to meet goals, objectives?
<--- Score

21. What changes could incentivize the right

organization to do more to prevent cyberattacks?
<--- Score

22. How are you going to measure success?
<--- Score

23. Do you need different testing techniques and other quality assurance measures for them?
<--- Score

24. What capabilities did each organization have to prevent the given cyberattack?
<--- Score

25. Is it organized by the needs of the user?
<--- Score

26. What does Secure coding success mean to the stakeholders?
<--- Score

27. Can information overload actually worsen the problem?
<--- Score

28. What is the problem with the preceding code?
<--- Score

29. Do your users have any special needs that will affect the resources selected?
<--- Score

30. When/where to find security issues?
<--- Score

31. Do you need to identify the attacker?

<--- Score

32. What situation(s) led to this Secure coding Self Assessment?
<--- Score

33. Do you have key management policies binding keys to identifiable owners?
<--- Score

34. How are the Secure coding's objectives aligned to the group's overall stakeholder strategy?
<--- Score

35. Does it solve the semantic mismatch problem better than other tools?
<--- Score

36. How much time, effort, and expertise is needed to exploit the threat?
<--- Score

37. What kinds of issues are raised by forms of security?
<--- Score

38. Will the cloud vendor meet your organizations computing and access needs?
<--- Score

39. What will happen in the event of a security breach?
<--- Score

40. Does the device likely need to meet any specific compliance requirements?

<--- Score

41. Are there any specific expectations or concerns about the Secure coding team, Secure coding itself?
<--- Score

42. Why do you need to know about PCI compliance?
<--- Score

43. How much are sponsors, customers, partners, stakeholders involved in Secure coding? In other words, what are the risks, if Secure coding does not deliver successfully?
<--- Score

44. What incentives did each organization have to prevent the given cyberattack?
<--- Score

45. How frequently does the user need to enter the security code?
<--- Score

46. Does the providers network have intrusion detection & prevention in place?
<--- Score

47. Do conditions exist that prevent logging or auditing?
<--- Score

Add up total points for this section:
_____ = Total points for this section

Divided by: ______ (number of

statements answered) = ______
Average score for this section

Transfer your score to the Secure coding Index at the beginning of the Self-Assessment.

CRITERION #2: DEFINE:

INTENT: Formulate the stakeholder problem. Define the problem, needs and objectives.

In my belief, the answer to this question is clearly defined:

5 Strongly Agree

4 Agree

3 Neutral

2 Disagree

1 Strongly Disagree

1. Does the server require or recommend remote access for manufacturer support?
<--- Score

2. Is the team sponsored by a champion or stakeholder leader?
<--- Score

3. Is there a critical path to deliver Secure coding

results?
<--- Score

4. Which would best meet your requirements?
<--- Score

5. What are the rough order estimates on cost savings/ opportunities that Secure coding brings?
<--- Score

6. Is the team equipped with available and reliable resources?
<--- Score

7. Does the application require certain files to be safe from public exposure?
<--- Score

8. What customer feedback methods were used to solicit their input?
<--- Score

9. Are most stakeholders reviewing vendor agreements for security requirements?
<--- Score

10. Are all security test requirements being met?
<--- Score

11. What critical content must be communicated – who, what, when, where, and how?
<--- Score

12. Are stakeholder processes mapped?
<--- Score

13. How do you keep key subject matter experts in the loop?
<--- Score

14. Will team members perform Secure coding work when assigned and in a timely fashion?
<--- Score

15. What is in scope for PCI requirements?
<--- Score

16. How is the team tracking and documenting its work?
<--- Score

17. Which test cases would best test a systems security procedure?
<--- Score

18. Have you traced your security requirements?
<--- Score

19. Will team members regularly document their Secure coding work?
<--- Score

20. What tool or tools do you use to manage requirements?
<--- Score

21. What are the business requirements driving the change?
<--- Score

22. How was the 'as is' process map developed, reviewed, verified and validated?

<--- Score

23. Is data collected and displayed to better understand customer(s) critical needs and requirements.
<--- Score

24. How did the Secure coding manager receive input to the development of a Secure coding improvement plan and the estimated completion dates/times of each activity?
<--- Score

25. Has everyone on the team, including the team leaders, been properly trained?
<--- Score

26. Which portions of the project will require threat models before release?
<--- Score

27. Is the team adequately staffed with the desired cross-functionality? If not, what additional resources are available to the team?
<--- Score

28. Are team charters developed?
<--- Score

29. Are there different segments of customers?
<--- Score

30. Are projects specifying some security tests based on requirements?
<--- Score

31. How does the Secure coding manager ensure against scope creep?
<--- Score

32. Has the Secure coding work been fairly and/or equitably divided and delegated among team members who are qualified and capable to perform the work? Has everyone contributed?
<--- Score

33. Is full participation by members in regularly held team meetings guaranteed?
<--- Score

34. Who are the Secure coding improvement team members, including Management Leads and Coaches?
<--- Score

35. When is the estimated completion date?
<--- Score

36. Do project teams pull requirements from best practices and compliance guidance?
<--- Score

37. Is Secure coding currently on schedule according to the plan?
<--- Score

38. What are the dynamics of the communication plan?
<--- Score

39. Is there a completed SIPOC representation, describing the Suppliers, Inputs, Process, Outputs, and

Customers?
<--- Score

40. Is there a Secure coding management charter, including stakeholder case, problem and goal statements, scope, milestones, roles and responsibilities, communication plan?
<--- Score

41. Is a fully trained team formed, supported, and committed to work on the Secure coding improvements?
<--- Score

42. What are the boundaries of the scope? What is in bounds and what is not? What is the start point? What is the stop point?
<--- Score

43. When are meeting minutes sent out? Who is on the distribution list?
<--- Score

44. When is/was the Secure coding start date?
<--- Score

45. Is the improvement team aware of the different versions of a process: what they think it is vs. what it actually is vs. what it should be vs. what it could be?
<--- Score

46. Has a high-level 'as is' process map been completed, verified and validated?
<--- Score

47. Are project teams specifying requirements

based on feedback from other security activities?
<--- Score

48. How often are the team meetings?
<--- Score

49. Is the Secure coding scope manageable?
<--- Score

50. Are overall legal requirements met?
<--- Score

51. What are the compelling stakeholder reasons for embarking on Secure coding?
<--- Score

52. Is feature required by most users?
<--- Score

53. Are customers identified and high impact areas defined?
<--- Score

54. What are the Roles and Responsibilities for each team member and its leadership? Where is this documented?
<--- Score

55. What firewall requirements are you faced with?
<--- Score

56. Has anyone else (internal or external to the group) attempted to solve this problem or a similar one before? If so, what knowledge can be leveraged from these previous efforts?
<--- Score

57. Are security test cases comprehensively generated for application specific logic?
<--- Score

58. Has a project plan, Gantt chart, or similar been developed/completed?
<--- Score

59. Is the team formed and are team leaders (Coaches and Management Leads) assigned?
<--- Score

60. Is there a completed, verified, and validated high-level 'as is' (not 'should be' or 'could be') stakeholder process map?
<--- Score

61. Are there any constraints known that bear on the ability to perform Secure coding work? How is the team addressing them?
<--- Score

62. Are customer(s) identified and segmented according to their different needs and requirements?
<--- Score

63. What information is required to reset the password?
<--- Score

64. Is the current 'as is' process being followed? If not, what are the discrepancies?
<--- Score

65. Are security requirements completed on

schedule?
<--- Score

66. Has the direction changed at all during the course of Secure coding? If so, when did it change and why?
<--- Score

67. What specifically is the problem? Where does it occur? When does it occur? What is its extent?
<--- Score

68. Are the security requirements specified by project teams being audited?
<--- Score

69. Have you followed the regulatory requirements?
<--- Score

70. What would be the goal or target for a Secure coding's improvement team?
<--- Score

71. What knowledge or experience is required?
<--- Score

72. Is there regularly 100% attendance at the team meetings? If not, have appointed substitutes attended to preserve cross-functionality and full representation?
<--- Score

73. What is the specific scope of the fuzz testing requirements?
<--- Score

74. Are improvement team members fully trained on Secure coding?
<--- Score

75. Are different versions of process maps needed to account for the different types of inputs?
<--- Score

76. What constraints exist that might impact the team?
<--- Score

77. Is the application required to authenticate each and every session?
<--- Score

78. Does the team have regular meetings?
<--- Score

79. Are the security requirements valid?
<--- Score

80. Is the work to date meeting requirements?
<--- Score

81. Has the improvement team collected the 'voice of the customer' (obtained feedback – qualitative and quantitative)?
<--- Score

82. Are all micro feature required by most users?
<--- Score

83. Are compliance requirements specifically considered by project teams?
<--- Score

84. What best defines your level of involvement in your organizations application security activities?
<--- Score

85. Do the problem and goal statements meet the SMART criteria (specific, measurable, attainable, relevant, and time-bound)?
<--- Score

86. How will variation in the actual durations of each activity be dealt with to ensure that the expected Secure coding results are met?
<--- Score

87. If substitutes have been appointed, have they been briefed on the Secure coding goals and received regular communications as to the progress to date?
<--- Score

88. Why should you take the time and effort required to make them secure?
<--- Score

89. Have the customer needs been translated into specific, measurable requirements? How?
<--- Score

90. What key stakeholder process output measure(s) does Secure coding leverage and how?
<--- Score

91. How will the Secure coding team and the group measure complete success of Secure coding?
<--- Score

92. What happens if the preservation requirements outlast the terms of the SLA?
<--- Score

93. Has a team charter been developed and communicated?
<--- Score

94. Is Secure coding linked to key stakeholder goals and objectives?
<--- Score

95. Does the system require special software?
<--- Score

96. What is the scope of the security critical functions, system, and software?
<--- Score

97. Has/have the customer(s) been identified?
<--- Score

Add up total points for this section:
_____ = Total points for this section

Divided by: ______ (number of statements answered) = ______ Average score for this section

Transfer your score to the Secure coding Index at the beginning of the Self-Assessment.

CRITERION #3: MEASURE:

INTENT: Gather the correct data.
Measure the current performance and evolution of the situation.

In my belief, the answer to this question is clearly defined:

5 Strongly Agree

4 Agree

3 Neutral

2 Disagree

1 Strongly Disagree

1. Are process variation components displayed/ communicated using suitable charts, graphs, plots?
<--- Score

2. What security measures are used?
<--- Score

3. How mature are your organizations processes for incident detection and analysis?

<--- Score

4. Is long term and short term variability accounted for?
<--- Score

5. How are cybersecurity maturity and compliance levels measured?
<--- Score

6. Does the design review process incorporate detailed data-level analysis?
<--- Score

7. Do you use multiple static analysis tools?
<--- Score

8. Are high impact defects defined and identified in the stakeholder process?
<--- Score

9. What are the current cybersecurity risk level and potential business impacts?
<--- Score

10. Do you use code analysis and/or secure programming tools in your work?
<--- Score

11. How much time and money will it cost to fix it?
<--- Score

12. What key measures identified indicate the performance of the stakeholder process?
<--- Score

13. How has GDPR impacted products and services offered?
<--- Score

14. What users will be impacted?
<--- Score

15. Can most project teams access automated code analysis tools to find security problems?
<--- Score

16. Why static instead of dynamic analysis?
<--- Score

17. What additional tools or resources are needed to detect, analyze, and mitigate future incidents?
<--- Score

18. Did you run all analysis tools, and when was the last run of the tools?
<--- Score

19. Which pointer analysis should you use?
<--- Score

20. What are the principles of static code analysis and how security code review should be employed?
<--- Score

21. What data was collected (past, present, future/ongoing)?
<--- Score

22. Do you use an automated source code analysis tool to detect security defects in code prior to

production?
<--- Score

23. Are the session ids provably resistant to statistical or cryptanalysis?
<--- Score

24. How large is the gap between current performance and the customer-specified (goal) performance?
<--- Score

25. What are the agreed upon definitions of the high impact areas, defect(s), unit(s), and opportunities that will figure into the process capability metrics?
<--- Score

26. What is the potential impact on your organization if the information is disclosed to unauthorized personnel?
<--- Score

27. How network configurations can impact internal code operations?
<--- Score

28. What is the impact of the user on the correctness of mappings?
<--- Score

29. What are the cybersecurity risks and potential business impacts to the prime business objectives?
<--- Score

30. What industry best describes your

organizations focus?
<--- Score

31. Are key measures identified and agreed upon?
<--- Score

32. Does management have the right priorities among projects?
<--- Score

33. How much pain would a buffer overflow vulnerability cause in your program?
<--- Score

34. Why you need data flow analysis?
<--- Score

35. What particular quality tools did the team find helpful in establishing measurements?
<--- Score

36. What is the recovery process, cost to recover?
<--- Score

37. Will a critical system disruption or a data theft cause a disruption to the business?
<--- Score

38. What is the Secure coding business impact?
<--- Score

39. What has the team done to assure the stability and accuracy of the measurement process?
<--- Score

40. Do most project teams specifically analyze

design elements for security mechanisms?
<--- Score

41. Does a change request require security impact analysis?
<--- Score

42. Who participated in the data collection for measurements?
<--- Score

43. Are adequate measures taken to maintain the integrity of the system?
<--- Score

44. How to analyze malware discovered as part of incident response or breach investigations?
<--- Score

45. What tools and techniques work in malware analysis?
<--- Score

46. Do you have qualified tools that support security analysis during development?
<--- Score

47. What would happen if you choose to narrow down your focus and concentrate only on software development?
<--- Score

48. Is key measure data collection planned and executed, process variation displayed and communicated and performance baselined?
<--- Score

49. Have you found any 'ground fruit' or 'low-hanging fruit' for immediate remedies to the gap in performance?
<--- Score

50. What is your approach to continuously implementing innovation and cost effective service delivery?
<--- Score

51. Is per-project data for cost of assurance activities collected?
<--- Score

52. How many data sources and systems can be impacted?
<--- Score

53. Does the design review process incorporate detailed data level analysis?
<--- Score

54. Do you see new threats to web applications negatively impacting your organization?
<--- Score

55. Is per project data for cost of assurance activities collected?
<--- Score

56. What are the key input variables? What are the key process variables? What are the key output variables?
<--- Score

57. Was a data collection plan established?

<--- Score

58. Do you use manual source code analysis to detect security defects in code prior to production?
<--- Score

59. Is Process Variation Displayed/Communicated?
<--- Score

60. Are the files within the web root?
<--- Score

61. Which method are you using to measure your product size?
<--- Score

62. Is data collected on key measures that were identified?
<--- Score

63. Is there a Performance Baseline?
<--- Score

64. Is the check applied on all the required files and folder within web root directory?
<--- Score

65. Is data collection planned and executed?
<--- Score

66. How does security fit in your priorities?
<--- Score

67. How long to keep data and how to manage retention costs?

<--- Score

68. What charts has the team used to display the components of variation in the process?
<--- Score

69. Is a solid data collection plan established that includes measurement systems analysis?
<--- Score

70. What tools and methods should be used to measure the defects?
<--- Score

71. How could a static analysis tool evaluate the assertion?
<--- Score

72. How can testing with static code analysis help?
<--- Score

Add up total points for this section:
_____ = Total points for this section

Divided by: ______ (number of statements answered) = ______
Average score for this section

Transfer your score to the Secure coding Index at the beginning of the Self-Assessment.

CRITERION #4: ANALYZE:

INTENT: Analyze causes, assumptions and hypotheses.

In my belief, the answer to this question is clearly defined:

5 Strongly Agree

4 Agree

3 Neutral

2 Disagree

1 Strongly Disagree

1. How will data be protected from intrusion or disasters?
<--- Score

2. Is storage in the data store set to a known value after use?
<--- Score

3. Were Pareto charts (or similar) used to portray the 'heavy hitters' (or key sources of variation)?

<--- Score

4. What does the data say about the performance of the stakeholder process?
<--- Score

5. Are most project utilizing a change management process that is well understood?
<--- Score

6. Why is sensitive data exposure dangerous?
<--- Score

7. Do you have qualified people, tools, and environments?
<--- Score

8. Do you have capability to recover data for a specific customer in the case of a failure or data loss?
<--- Score

9. How secure does the data need to be?
<--- Score

10. What are the processes for audit reporting and management?
<--- Score

11. What quality tools were used to get through the analyze phase?
<--- Score

12. Did the switch manufacturer follow industry best practices in the development process?
<--- Score

13. Do most projects consistently collect and report data and metrics related to incidents?
<--- Score

14. Which describes the acceptable amount of data loss measured in time?
<--- Score

15. What tools were used to generate the list of possible causes?
<--- Score

16. Will the service accept resources with/without specific metadata?
<--- Score

17. Has the data been updated recently?
<--- Score

18. Is the database is on another host?
<--- Score

19. Do you view any sensitive data that should be protected?
<--- Score

20. Will data be collocated with other customers data?
<--- Score

21. Do you have technical control capabilities to enforce tenant data retention policies?
<--- Score

22. Have you modified your process to detect new

potential threats?
<--- Score

23. Is all access to the data store throttled through one entry point?
<--- Score

24. Do you need a key management application to do a crypto erase on your drives?
<--- Score

25. What staff has access to the production databases?
<--- Score

26. Are most roles in the development process given role- specific training and guidance?
<--- Score

27. Why is the application sending out data?
<--- Score

28. What logical or physical separation exists to protect each clients data from others?
<--- Score

29. How do you manage the keys for all your data center systems and the endpoint devices?
<--- Score

30. When should a process be art not science?
<--- Score

31. Does the system contain sensitive data that must be protected from change?
<--- Score

32. Do your data management policies and procedures address tenant and service level conflicts of interests?
<--- Score

33. When the data store is full, is data written to the beginning of the data store?
<--- Score

34. What data is stored on and generated by the device?
<--- Score

35. How mature are your organizations processes for incident handling?
<--- Score

36. Are the responsibilities regarding data stewardship defined, assigned, documented and communicated?
<--- Score

37. Does data collector require an employees user name and password to be different?
<--- Score

38. Do you have control about who can see which data returned from your BI tools?
<--- Score

39. What Secure coding data will be collected?
<--- Score

40. Is the data entry operator using the admin password?

<--- Score

41. How will corresponding data be collected?
<--- Score

42. Have all user groups and related data privacy needs been identified and documented?
<--- Score

43. Are there any constraints on the selection process?
<--- Score

44. What were the crucial 'moments of truth' on the process map?
<--- Score

45. What Secure coding data should be managed?
<--- Score

46. Where are your data centers based?
<--- Score

47. How is the log in process protected?
<--- Score

48. Does data collector have a procedure for customers wishing to file a grievance or complaint?
<--- Score

49. Is the data sent on encrypted channel?
<--- Score

50. Who stores the ever changing data?
<--- Score

51. Is there any sensitive data in configuration files?
<--- Score

52. Does the organization utilize a consistent process for incident reporting and handling?
<--- Score

53. How would you be harmed if the information/ data were unexpectedly changed?
<--- Score

54. What information is generated by, consumed by, processed on, stored in, and retrieved by the application?
<--- Score

55. Are gaps between current performance and the goal performance identified?
<--- Score

56. Is storage in the data store set to a known value before use?
<--- Score

57. Did any value-added analysis or 'lean thinking' take place to identify some of the gaps shown on the 'as is' process map?
<--- Score

58. Are you using a complete development process?
<--- Score

59. Were any designed experiments used to generate

additional insight into the data analysis?
<--- Score

60. Is pii going to be stored/processed by the cloud services?
<--- Score

61. Is there a requirement to encrypt certain data?
<--- Score

62. Does the application connect to the database using an encrypted link?
<--- Score

63. What tools were used to narrow the list of possible causes?
<--- Score

64. Has the data been modified during retrieval, in transit, or in storage?
<--- Score

65. Is the performance gap determined?
<--- Score

66. Is data and process analysis, root cause analysis and quantifying the gap/opportunity in place?
<--- Score

67. Do you ensure the destruction and removal of data in accordance with policy?
<--- Score

68. Do you review all agreements, policies and processes at least annually?
<--- Score

69. Who will facilitate the team and process?
<--- Score

70. Do you have tools to collect logs and metadata from the cloud platform?
<--- Score

71. What is wrong with sensitive data here?
<--- Score

72. Does it store the session in memory, on disk, or in a database?
<--- Score

73. Were there any improvement opportunities identified from the process analysis?
<--- Score

74. Can the process for maximizing the accounts capabilities be forced or socially engineered?
<--- Score

75. How does the system provide output?
<--- Score

76. How do you establish trust in the data?
<--- Score

77. How would you be harmed if the process or function failed to provide expected results?
<--- Score

78. What systems/processes must you excel at?
<--- Score

79. How do you best fit into your existing process?
<--- Score

80. Do the memory free routines erase the data?
<--- Score

81. Does your organization utilize a consistent process for incident reporting and handling?
<--- Score

82. Does data collector destroy media when it is no longer needed for business or legal reasons?
<--- Score

83. Are most roles in the development process given role specific training and guidance?
<--- Score

84. How is your organizations data segregated from that of other clients?
<--- Score

85. Is there a risk related to data location?
<--- Score

86. How are users and processes authenticated?
<--- Score

87. Do you collect capacity and use data for all relevant components of your cloud service offering?
<--- Score

88. How is your organizations data disposed of at the time of contract termination?
<--- Score

89. Does data collector have a risk assessment process in place?
<--- Score

90. How will the servers be used to process data?
<--- Score

91. Is the Secure coding process severely broken such that a re-design is necessary?
<--- Score

92. Have the problem and goal statements been updated to reflect the additional knowledge gained from the analyze phase?
<--- Score

93. What conclusions were drawn from the team's data collection and analysis? How did the team reach these conclusions?
<--- Score

94. What other controls are in place to ensure there is no mix of each of your clients data?
<--- Score

95. What is the cost of poor quality as supported by the team's analysis?
<--- Score

96. What would be the best way to test your strategy once you agree on the process?
<--- Score

97. Was a cause-and-effect diagram used to explore the different types of causes (or sources of variation)?

<--- Score

98. Where is the data center located?
<--- Score

99. How do attackers exploit sensitive data exposure?
<--- Score

100. Is a consistent process used to apply upgrades and patches to critical dependencies?
<--- Score

101. What were the financial benefits resulting from any 'ground fruit or low-hanging fruit' (quick fixes)?
<--- Score

102. Is code signing routinely performed on software components using a consistent process?
<--- Score

103. Have any additional benefits been identified that will result from closing all or most of the gaps?
<--- Score

104. What is the correctness of the automated mappings generated by the plugin?
<--- Score

105. What are the data backup policies and procedures?
<--- Score

106. How will the data be checked for quality?
<--- Score

107. How is data used for program management and improvement?
<--- Score

108. How long are backups and operating data retained?
<--- Score

109. What are the revised rough estimates of the financial savings/opportunity for Secure coding improvements?
<--- Score

110. Did any additional data need to be collected?
<--- Score

111. Does the application connect to the database using low privilege users?
<--- Score

112. Does the application use background / batch / scheduled processes to work on user supplied data?
<--- Score

113. What did the team gain from developing a sub-process map?
<--- Score

114. Is the documented process for file signing under dual control being followed?
<--- Score

115. Are test data and accounts removed before production systems become active?
<--- Score

116. What can happen to your sensitive data?
<--- Score

117. Does your application query a database?
<--- Score

118. Is the data accessible by users at all times?
<--- Score

119. Was a detailed process map created to amplify critical steps of the 'as is' stakeholder process?
<--- Score

120. Do you view sensitive data that should be protected?
<--- Score

121. Is there any way to speed up the process?
<--- Score

122. When the data store is full, is data discarded?
<--- Score

123. Are most roles in the development process given role-specific training and guidance?
<--- Score

124. Is the gap/opportunity displayed and communicated in financial terms?
<--- Score

125. Can the user enter commands into the Data input field?
<--- Score

126. What privileges are required by the software at each step of the process?
<--- Score

127. Are users within your Auditable Unit permitted to send or receive sensitive data via email?
<--- Score

128. Is all data protected adequately in transit?
<--- Score

129. Are there data retained for forensics?
<--- Score

130. Are there any risks that people should know about the setup process?
<--- Score

131. How was the detailed process map generated, verified, and validated?
<--- Score

132. What are the Secure coding design outputs?
<--- Score

133. Do your applications non administrative users interact with elevated processes as services?
<--- Score

Add up total points for this section:
_____ = Total points for this section

Divided by: ______ (number of statements answered) = ______ Average score for this section

Transfer your score to the Secure coding Index at the beginning of the Self-Assessment.

CRITERION #5: IMPROVE:

INTENT: Develop a practical solution. Innovate, establish and test the solution and to measure the results.

In my belief, the answer to this question is clearly defined:

5 Strongly Agree

4 Agree

3 Neutral

2 Disagree

1 Strongly Disagree

1. How do you ensure development of secure application?
<--- Score

2. What does the 'should be' process map/design look like?
<--- Score

3. Is reduced compile time optimization an

acceptable trade off for increased safety?
<--- Score

4. Is there a small-scale pilot for proposed improvement(s)? What conclusions were drawn from the outcomes of a pilot?
<--- Score

5. How did the team generate the list of possible solutions?
<--- Score

6. How does the solution remove the key sources of issues discovered in the analyze phase?
<--- Score

7. What are the best development practices to correct errors?
<--- Score

8. Are the key business and technology risks being managed?
<--- Score

9. What is Secure coding risk?
<--- Score

10. What tools were used to tap into the creativity and encourage 'outside the box' thinking?
<--- Score

11. What is the current progress of evidence development?
<--- Score

12. What tools were used to evaluate the potential

solutions?
<--- Score

13. What tests have been and will be run to understand inherent software security risks?
<--- Score

14. What assumptions are made about the solution and approach?
<--- Score

15. Is the Secure coding solution sustainable?
<--- Score

16. Why is software development so hard?
<--- Score

17. What is the team's contingency plan for potential problems occurring in implementation?
<--- Score

18. What does your risk posture look like now?
<--- Score

19. What strategies are in in place to identify and manage the Cybersecurity risks to the ICS?
<--- Score

20. Are improved process ('should be') maps modified based on pilot data and analysis?
<--- Score

21. Is a solution implementation plan established, including schedule/work breakdown structure, resources, risk management plan, cost/budget, and control plan?

<--- Score

22. How do users discover new tools in software development and beyond?
<--- Score

23. Are security related alerts and error conditions documented for most projects?
<--- Score

24. What error proofing will be done to address some of the discrepancies observed in the 'as is' process?
<--- Score

25. How will application security and application development environments evolve over time?
<--- Score

26. Were any criteria developed to assist the team in testing and evaluating potential solutions?
<--- Score

27. Are all requirements and trust levels for customers access defined and documented?
<--- Score

28. Do project teams specifically consider risk from external software?
<--- Score

29. How is continuous improvement applied to risk management?
<--- Score

30. Why web application risks occur?
<--- Score

31. Is there a cost/benefit analysis of optimal solution(s)?
<--- Score

32. Does your product provide value in the market place while limiting risk to acquirers and users?
<--- Score

33. How is knowledge sharing about risk management improved?
<--- Score

34. How can OWASP assist mobile developers?
<--- Score

35. How could information sharing with other organizations have been improved?
<--- Score

36. Was a pilot designed for the proposed solution(s)?
<--- Score

37. Do you have the optimal project management team structure?
<--- Score

38. How do you gauge the strengths and weaknesses of your development team?
<--- Score

39. Describe the design of the pilot and what tests were conducted, if any?
<--- Score

40. What information online can put you at risk?

<--- Score

41. What is your software development lifecycle?
<--- Score

42. Are risk ratings used to tailor the required assurance activities?
<--- Score

43. Are project teams generally performing review of selected high risk code?
<--- Score

44. What were the underlying assumptions on the cost-benefit analysis?
<--- Score

45. Are possible solutions generated and tested?
<--- Score

46. Who oversees and is responsible for your platforms development services?
<--- Score

47. Does your security strategy address new technology risks?
<--- Score

48. Does your CISO and/or application development director have a login?
<--- Score

49. Do you believe mobile apps affect your organizations application security risk profile?
<--- Score

50. Do you have a documented, organization wide program in place to manage risk?
<--- Score

51. Are most of your applications and resources categorized by risk?
<--- Score

52. What is the likelihood that the threat will initiate the risk?
<--- Score

53. What communications are necessary to support the implementation of the solution?
<--- Score

54. Can you integrate quality management and risk management?
<--- Score

55. What were the key requirements for a cloud based IAM solution?
<--- Score

56. Do project teams document the attack perimeter of software designs?
<--- Score

57. Have you used secure programming principles and practices in software development?
<--- Score

58. Who are the Secure coding decision-makers?
<--- Score

59. Do most of the business stakeholders

understand your organizations risk profile?
<--- Score

60. What security risks are covered by financial means?
<--- Score

61. Is there any other Secure coding solution?
<--- Score

62. What types of vulnerabilities do developers introduce?
<--- Score

63. Which is an important aspect of security test results?
<--- Score

64. Is the security of outsourced code improving, remaining the same, or getting worse?
<--- Score

65. Who are the Secure coding decision makers?
<--- Score

66. Is Secure coding documentation maintained?
<--- Score

67. Does your organization understand and document the types of attackers it faces?
<--- Score

68. Do you have documented ownership for each stage of the lifecycle of encryption keys?
<--- Score

69. Who manages supplier risk management in your organization?
<--- Score

70. Are new and improved process ('should be') maps developed?
<--- Score

71. What are the common security concerns of developers?
<--- Score

72. Is pilot data collected and analyzed?
<--- Score

73. How are administrators alerted when security risk score rises?
<--- Score

74. Does routine project audit require a baseline for design review results?
<--- Score

75. Does most of your organization know about what is required based on risk ratings?
<--- Score

76. Do the majority of projects document some requirements for the operational environment?
<--- Score

77. What are the Secure coding security risks?
<--- Score

78. Can the application revert back to normal operation when the security risk score drops to

normal levels?
<--- Score

79. Which percentage of overall vulnerabilities are high risk?
<--- Score

80. Do the viable solutions scale to future needs?
<--- Score

81. Are procedures documented for managing Secure coding risks?
<--- Score

82. Are projects using automation to evaluate security test cases?
<--- Score

83. Why is it important to reassess security risk expectations on a frequent basis?
<--- Score

84. Do you believe cloud based applications affect your organizations security risk profile?
<--- Score

85. Are security-related alerts and error conditions documented for most projects?
<--- Score

86. Are the risks fully understood, reasonable and manageable?
<--- Score

87. Is the optimal solution selected based on testing and analysis?

<--- Score

88. Are all firewall access control lists documented with business justification?
<--- Score

89. Are risk management tasks balanced centrally and locally?
<--- Score

90. Is there significant variation in code review effectiveness between developers?
<--- Score

91. What are there internal security evaluations?
<--- Score

92. Does each project team have access to secure development best practices and guidance?
<--- Score

93. Is the implementation plan designed?
<--- Score

94. What is Secure coding's impact on utilizing the best solution(s)?
<--- Score

95. Do most projects in your organization consider and document likely threats?
<--- Score

96. What are the key security risks within the application?
<--- Score

97. How are the developers trying to protect the application?
<--- Score

98. What tools were most useful during the improve phase?
<--- Score

99. Are the most efficient solutions problem-specific?
<--- Score

100. Is the resource improved and enlarged and updated appropriately?
<--- Score

101. Can the change be modified that the risk is reduced?
<--- Score

102. Are project teams generally performing review of selected high-risk code?
<--- Score

103. How will the team or the process owner(s) monitor the implementation plan to see that it is working as intended?
<--- Score

104. How do you address the risks and harness the benefits for security in AI software?
<--- Score

105. What alternative responses are available to manage risk?
<--- Score

106. What is the implementation plan?
<--- Score

107. Which access policy rules were used as a basis for a decision?
<--- Score

108. Is a contingency plan established?
<--- Score

109. Are there any constraints (technical, political, cultural, or otherwise) that would inhibit certain solutions?
<--- Score

110. Why security during development?
<--- Score

111. How is software development organized?
<--- Score

112. What are risks, threats, and vulnerabilities what is malicious software?
<--- Score

113. Are the best solutions selected?
<--- Score

114. Has the developer made assumptions that an attacker could violate?
<--- Score

115. How to efficiently ensure the security of software increments produced by development iterations?
<--- Score

116. Are all protection mechanisms and controls captured and mapped back to threats?
<--- Score

117. Have most developers been given high level security awareness training?
<--- Score

118. What lessons, if any, from a pilot were incorporated into the design of the full-scale solution?
<--- Score

119. Which is a potential security risk?
<--- Score

120. How will the group know that the solution worked?
<--- Score

121. What risks would a successful attack pose to your organization?
<--- Score

122. Has your auditable unit developed its own web based applications?
<--- Score

123. What attendant changes will need to be made to ensure that the solution is successful?
<--- Score

124. How effective are developers at security code review?
<--- Score

Add up total points for this section:
_____ = Total points for this section

Divided by: ______ (number of statements answered) = ______ Average score for this section

Transfer your score to the Secure coding Index at the beginning of the Self-Assessment.

CRITERION #6: CONTROL:

INTENT: Implement the practical solution. Maintain the performance and correct possible complications.

In my belief, the answer to this question is clearly defined:

5 Strongly Agree

4 Agree

3 Neutral

2 Disagree

1 Strongly Disagree

1. What should the next improvement project be that is related to Secure coding?
<--- Score

2. Does job training on the documented procedures need to be part of the process team's education and training?
<--- Score

3. What tests will be performed against the systems during a scan?
<--- Score

4. How is remote server access controlled?
<--- Score

5. What quality control procedures does the producer employ?
<--- Score

6. Is a response plan in place for when the input, process, or output measures indicate an 'out-of-control' condition?
<--- Score

7. What are planned effort requirements by specialty?
<--- Score

8. What is the recommended frequency of auditing?
<--- Score

9. What quality tools were useful in the control phase?
<--- Score

10. Do project teams utilize automation to check code against application specific coding standards?
<--- Score

11. What can an attacker learn based on how the application responds?
<--- Score

12. Have you tested your security incident

response plans in the last year?
<--- Score

13. Do the provider services offer fine grained access control?
<--- Score

14. How comprehensive is the ICS incident response plan?
<--- Score

15. Are suggested corrective/restorative actions indicated on the response plan for known causes to problems that might surface?
<--- Score

16. Is knowledge gained on process shared and institutionalized?
<--- Score

17. Is there a documented and implemented monitoring plan?
<--- Score

18. Do access control systems have a default deny all setting?
<--- Score

19. Is reporting being used or needed?
<--- Score

20. Have the security controls been implemented, or is there an implementation plan in place?
<--- Score

21. How will the day-to-day responsibilities for

monitoring and continual improvement be transferred from the improvement team to the process owner?
<--- Score

22. Have you followed your organizations standard process model?
<--- Score

23. Has the improved process and its steps been standardized?
<--- Score

24. Is software development driven by certain standards?
<--- Score

25. What media/tools or sources do you prefer to use while learning new things related to programming?
<--- Score

26. What internal personnel controls are used?
<--- Score

27. Is the static content access controlled using the current logged in user?
<--- Score

28. Are projects periodically audited to ensure a baseline of compliance with policies and standards?
<--- Score

29. How far ahead does your security strategy plan?

<--- Score

30. Are documented procedures clear and easy to follow for the operators?
<--- Score

31. Do you apply per zone access control rights?
<--- Score

32. Which pieces of input to the program can an attacker control?
<--- Score

33. How long will it take to perform security testing given planned resources and scope?
<--- Score

34. How will input, process, and output variables be checked to detect for sub-optimal conditions?
<--- Score

35. What are advantages to imposing security standards in contracts?
<--- Score

36. Does the response plan contain a definite closed loop continual improvement scheme (e.g., plan-do-check-act)?
<--- Score

37. Does request originate from your organization controlled user device?
<--- Score

38. Can the provider give reports for monitoring user access?

<--- Score

39. Do project teams check software designs against known security risks?
<--- Score

40. Is the referrer code simple and robust against all forms of user attack?
<--- Score

41. Are operating procedures consistent?
<--- Score

42. Does each non anonymous entry point have an access control check?
<--- Score

43. Is a response plan established and deployed?
<--- Score

44. How is access control handled to the system?
<--- Score

45. How might the group capture best practices and lessons learned so as to leverage improvements?
<--- Score

46. What other systems, operations, processes, and infrastructures (hiring practices, staffing, training, incentives/rewards, metrics/dashboards/scorecards, etc.) need updates, additions, changes, or deletions in order to facilitate knowledge transfer and improvements?
<--- Score

47. Is there any form of quality control?

<--- Score

48. Does your organization utilize a set of policies and standards to control software development?
<--- Score

49. Does the cloud service provider have necessary security controls on human resources?
<--- Score

50. Is code validated against % of applications rated security coding standards?
<--- Score

51. What coverage is obtained by the use of the custom authentication controls?
<--- Score

52. Is there documentation that will support the successful operation of the improvement?
<--- Score

53. Does the Secure coding performance meet the customer's requirements?
<--- Score

54. What have you learned from your many years of experience in the security industry?
<--- Score

55. How will report readings be checked to effectively monitor performance?
<--- Score

56. Does it use standard multimedia formats?
<--- Score

57. Who is the Secure coding process owner?
<--- Score

58. How is access control / key deployment auditable?
<--- Score

59. Is there a standardized process?
<--- Score

60. Is your privacy policy aligned with industry standards?
<--- Score

61. Are new process steps, standards, and documentation ingrained into normal operations?
<--- Score

62. Do you control inter zone communication?
<--- Score

63. Are there documented procedures?
<--- Score

64. Is there a control plan in place for sustaining improvements (short and long-term)?
<--- Score

65. Does each requirement trace to a specific test in the plan?
<--- Score

66. How strong is the system against known attacks?
<--- Score

67. Do project teams utilize automation to check code against application-specific coding standards?
<--- Score

68. What other areas of the group might benefit from the Secure coding team's improvements, knowledge, and learning?
<--- Score

69. Is there a recommended audit plan for routine surveillance inspections of Secure coding's gains?
<--- Score

70. Is all xml input data validated against an agreed schema?
<--- Score

71. What security measurement practices and data does your organization use to assist product planning?
<--- Score

72. Are project teams able to request an audit for compliance with policies and standards?
<--- Score

73. Where did you learn of it from a respected source?
<--- Score

74. Is new knowledge gained imbedded in the response plan?
<--- Score

75. How powerful are run time monitors with static information?
<--- Score

76. Have new or revised work instructions resulted?
<--- Score

77. Will any special training be provided for results interpretation?
<--- Score

78. Does a troubleshooting guide exist or is it needed?
<--- Score

79. Do you have a documented security incident response plan?
<--- Score

80. What are the critical parameters to watch?
<--- Score

81. What would a competitor do with a rivals business plan?
<--- Score

82. Do you use secure software development standards in your work?
<--- Score

83. What controls are implemented and enforced that protect user credentials and ensure a secure login procedure?
<--- Score

84. Does the organization utilize a set of policies and standards to control software development?

<--- Score

85. How do attackers exploit insufficient logging and monitoring?
<--- Score

86. Is there a transfer of ownership and knowledge to process owner and process team tasked with the responsibilities.
<--- Score

87. How will the process owner verify improvement in present and future sigma levels, process capabilities?
<--- Score

88. Which is a benefit of conforming to security testing standards?
<--- Score

89. What is the control/monitoring plan?
<--- Score

90. Where are spigit production servers located, and how is access to your assets and/or information controlled, physically secured, and restricted solely to authorized staff?
<--- Score

91. Where does windows Azure access control fit in?
<--- Score

92. How will the process owner and team be able to hold the gains?
<--- Score

93. How will new or emerging customer needs/ requirements be checked/communicated to orient the process toward meeting the new specifications and continually reducing variation?
<--- Score

94. Does your organization systematically use audits to collect and control compliance evidence?
<--- Score

95. What motivates you to learn about new programming techniques or languages?
<--- Score

96. Does the outsourced team understand your security goals and standards?
<--- Score

97. What guidelines and standards are available to you?
<--- Score

98. Why are some departments unwilling to implement controls for least privilege?
<--- Score

99. Do you integrate customized tenant requirements into your security incident response plans?
<--- Score

100. What key inputs and outputs are being measured on an ongoing basis?
<--- Score

101. Are most stakeholders reviewing access

control matrices for relevant projects?
<--- Score

Add up total points for this section:
_____ = Total points for this section

Divided by: ______ (number of statements answered) = ______ Average score for this section

Transfer your score to the Secure coding Index at the beginning of the Self-Assessment.

CRITERION #7: SUSTAIN:

INTENT: Retain the benefits.

In my belief, the answer to this question is clearly defined:

5 Strongly Agree

4 Agree

3 Neutral

2 Disagree

1 Strongly Disagree

1. Is it from an authoritative source?
<--- Score

2. How much system downtime does your organization tolerate?
<--- Score

3. Is access free and unrestricted?
<--- Score

4. What is the number of current/potential users

that you will be supporting?
<--- Score

5. What percentage of software projects meet time commitments?
<--- Score

6. How would you be harmed if the asset were unavailable for a period of time?
<--- Score

7. Is the information current and up to date?
<--- Score

8. How do relate to the most common vulnerabilities?
<--- Score

9. Does the threat model cover the actual usage scenarios and features of the product?
<--- Score

10. How will you stop supporting the software?
<--- Score

11. What information should be considered private?
<--- Score

12. Is there a good business reason why?
<--- Score

13. How do you know how good are the tools?
<--- Score

14. Does the material have any relation to other

works?
<--- Score

15. What effect can an individual with carte blanc access to all critical functions of a system have?
<--- Score

16. How does your billing system count the number of apps tested?
<--- Score

17. Does your feature listen on network sockets?
<--- Score

18. Is physical and logical user access to audit logs restricted to authorized personnel?
<--- Score

19. Have you registered with the Selective Service System?
<--- Score

20. Are users made aware of responsibilities for leaving unattended equipment in a secure manner?
<--- Score

21. Does your organization have an assigned security response team?
<--- Score

22. How can selection be applied to resource descriptions created by gathering software?
<--- Score

23. Does your byod policy specify the user roles

that are allowed access via a byod enabled device?
<--- Score

24. Are companies allowed to design effective security for systems?
<--- Score

25. Is the previous program vulnerable?
<--- Score

26. Are the characteristics of users and of typical usage mentioned?
<--- Score

27. Do people follow jobs or do jobs follow people?
<--- Score

28. How do you bring security into DevOps?
<--- Score

29. Are resources that contain advertising acceptable?
<--- Score

30. How will you differentiate between must fix versus should fix vulnerabilities?
<--- Score

31. Are most project stakeholders aware of how to obtain a formal design review?
<--- Score

32. How do attackers exploit authentication vulnerabilities?
<--- Score

33. What does security assurance look for your organization in cloud?
<--- Score

34. Does the system track how many failed login attempts a user has experienced?
<--- Score

35. Will an independent outsider be hired to perform an unbiased software security assessment?
<--- Score

36. Is it acceptable for it to come from an anonymous user?
<--- Score

37. Is the aim and purpose of the resource obvious at first sight?
<--- Score

38. What areas of the application will likely attract the attention of an attacker?
<--- Score

39. Are the individual Web pages concise or do you have to scroll forever?
<--- Score

40. Which xerox remote print services software is most secure?
<--- Score

41. Are time sensitive resources available in near real time?

<--- Score

42. How well did staff and management perform in dealing with the incident?
<--- Score

43. Are sources of the information stated?
<--- Score

44. Do you have separate key management and key usage duties?
<--- Score

45. Are all the external interfaces of the software explicitly mentioned?
<--- Score

46. Do you provide a supportive resource that is non obtrusive and easy to navigate?
<--- Score

47. How does the application maintain security?
<--- Score

48. Are any credits or compensation provided to independent vulnerability researchers?
<--- Score

49. Does the application implement any security mechanisms as authentication or authorization?
<--- Score

50. Are there any price limits in terms of the access charge?
<--- Score

51. What to look for when performing a code review?
<--- Score

52. Which is a main disadvantage to malware scanning tools?
<--- Score

53. How do you determine the number of apps that may be tested at any one time?
<--- Score

54. Is it easy to search the resource?
<--- Score

55. Do you use code reviews in your work?
<--- Score

56. Will the offering handle sensitive private information?
<--- Score

57. Is all management activity recorded?
<--- Score

58. Which refers to a series of characters used to verify a users identity?
<--- Score

59. What are the benefits of riscure training services?
<--- Score

60. How deep into the infrastructure can the threat agent go?
<--- Score

61. Does your application support an older and less secure authentication scheme?
<--- Score

62. What elements of the Session IDs are time linked?
<--- Score

63. Do you use dedicated secure networks to provide management access to your cloud service infrastructure?
<--- Score

64. When should your organization perform code reviews or penetration testing?
<--- Score

65. Will the application give access to the project?
<--- Score

66. What type of defects lead to security vulnerabilities?
<--- Score

67. How does security testing fit into your organization?
<--- Score

68. What is available via other information sources?
<--- Score

69. What sorts of techniques might an attacker use to subvert the application?
<--- Score

70. How do you know what is contained in the merging/acquired organizations source code?
<--- Score

71. Do you view a valid users credentials on the wire or in persistent storage?
<--- Score

72. Is the resource indexed electronically?
<--- Score

73. Do you have to avoid high business activity times?
<--- Score

74. Can the device withstand normal network vulnerability scanning?
<--- Score

75. How would a security breach affect the credibility of your organization?
<--- Score

76. Are project teams being audited for usage of secure architecture components?
<--- Score

77. How is cybersecurity different for medical devices?
<--- Score

78. What happens when security fails?
<--- Score

79. How will your code and applications react

when something has gone wrong?
<--- Score

80. Is secure programming enforced through organizational policies and rules?
<--- Score

81. Why is there still so much poor quality software around?
<--- Score

82. What are key attributes of security authentication of a medium complexity IT system?
<--- Score

83. What are the trends that weaken or strengthen your organization of application security in the future?
<--- Score

84. Is a date given stating when the web item was mounted?
<--- Score

85. Are logs kept of device or server access?
<--- Score

86. Is the information being maintained/updated?
<--- Score

87. Is it able to classify correctly vulnerabilities independently of class?
<--- Score

88. Is the information unique within the context of the total collection or does it duplicate?

<--- Score

89. Do you advertise shared security services with guidance for project teams?
<--- Score

90. Does the system have an effective search facility?
<--- Score

91. How do attackers trigger xml injections?
<--- Score

92. Are the application audit records vulnerable to unauthorised deletion, modification or disclosure?
<--- Score

93. Are vulnerabilities reduced to an acceptable level for release?
<--- Score

94. Are the logs for failed authentication attempts tied to a brute force mechanism?
<--- Score

95. Do you deliver security notes with the majority of software releases?
<--- Score

96. Do the logs contain sensitive information?
<--- Score

97. Does your organization have people with appropriate security testing skills?
<--- Score

98. Do you support the ability to force password changes upon first logon?
<--- Score

99. Do all of the cloud providers facilities have the same levels of security?
<--- Score

100. Are there any hard coded passwords or keys embedded in the program source?
<--- Score

101. What removes the most defects in the shortest time or least effort?
<--- Score

102. Will your application be secure enough when robots produce code for you?
<--- Score

103. Are there any logical gaps of information?
<--- Score

104. Do you concentrate on proper system design, common system failures, or some mixture?
<--- Score

105. Is there any known flaw(s) in APIs/Technology used?
<--- Score

106. Have a security team / organize it?
<--- Score

107. What assets matter to you as your organization?

<--- Score

108. Is any part of the product network facing?
<--- Score

109. Do you perform, at minimum, annual reviews to your privacy and security policies?
<--- Score

110. What exactly are you able to make the application do?
<--- Score

111. Does the system have a search facility?
<--- Score

112. Why do other organizations pay white hack hackers?
<--- Score

113. What will you do with the information once it is obtained?
<--- Score

114. How confident are you that your organization can architect around failures in your detection system?
<--- Score

115. What is the coverage in the collection?
<--- Score

116. Does your application support undo or recovery operations?
<--- Score

117. Is there a description of the update frequencies for the resources?
<--- Score

118. What functions should tools share?
<--- Score

119. Where do you start with security?
<--- Score

120. Does your application parse files?
<--- Score

121. Why old software can become insecure?
<--- Score

122. What kinds of organizations do you belong to?
<--- Score

123. Is there adequate maintenance of the information content?
<--- Score

124. Does the application generate or allow access to static content?
<--- Score

125. What ability does the provider have to deal with denial of service attacks?
<--- Score

126. Is there any information missing?
<--- Score

127. Which security activity is most effective in

finding vulnerabilities?
<--- Score

128. How is the information being used?
<--- Score

129. Are only authorized devices and software on the network?
<--- Score

130. What surprises do identical twins have for identity science?
<--- Score

131. How exploitable are the vulnerabilities?
<--- Score

132. Do its corrections interfere with the normal behavior of applications?
<--- Score

133. What happens if vendor goes bankrupt or out of business?
<--- Score

134. Where do you draw the line when considering security systems?
<--- Score

135. Will there be any kind of attack if your website is linking to some external websites?
<--- Score

136. Why should you choose your organization?
<--- Score

137. Can an administrator or other user provision accounts with privileges greater than own?
<--- Score

138. Does the network provide the customer with logging and notification?
<--- Score

139. How would you be harmed if an employee of your cloud provider accessed the asset?
<--- Score

140. Are most stakeholders able to pull in security coaches for use on projects?
<--- Score

141. Do you scan all systems or just critical assets?
<--- Score

142. What service levels will be offered?
<--- Score

143. Is there any original information?
<--- Score

144. Is the information of a type that has a limited period of use?
<--- Score

145. What programming language do you work with most in your organization?
<--- Score

146. How much application downtime does your organization tolerate?
<--- Score

147. How much information should the caller receive?
<--- Score

148. Is there any mention of the resource being available in another format?
<--- Score

149. What is the mission of your organization?
<--- Score

150. Is the resource currently accessible?
<--- Score

151. What are the entry points to interface with the system?
<--- Score

152. Do project teams use a method of rating threats for relative comparison?
<--- Score

153. Do you maintain key management procedures?
<--- Score

154. How will a breach of your system affect your installed base?
<--- Score

155. How often does your organization test applications for threats and vulnerabilities?
<--- Score

156. Which vulnerabilities will you respond to?

<--- Score

157. Will details on the security functionality be part of the final deliverables?
<--- Score

158. Are your encryption keys maintained by the cloud consumer or a trusted key management provider?
<--- Score

159. Why do smart people write buggy software?
<--- Score

160. What is security in your organization?
<--- Score

161. Why does your organizations applications contain vulnerable code?
<--- Score

162. Who pushed vendors toward better security?
<--- Score

163. What is the depth of the information?
<--- Score

164. Does the application have a mechanism to terminate the account?
<--- Score

165. Are you reviewing for security, functionality, maintainability, and/or style?
<--- Score

166. Is finding security holes a good idea?

<--- Score

167. How superficial/exhaustive is the information?
<--- Score

168. Is the server operating system hardened?
<--- Score

169. Do most project stakeholders know projects compliance status?
<--- Score

170. What are the challenges you face in recruiting and training cybersecurity department?
<--- Score

171. Does the information appear to be well researched?
<--- Score

172. When is the latest acceptable end date for the overall project?
<--- Score

173. Is the information peer reviewed?
<--- Score

174. Is customer network access separated from provider network access?
<--- Score

175. Does your organization use any technologies to enhance its security posture?
<--- Score

176. How does your organization assess the efficiency and effectiveness of information security?
<--- Score

177. What are the different types of penetration test?
<--- Score

178. Does the information appear to be valid, and well researched?
<--- Score

179. Will you migrate users to a new version?
<--- Score

180. What type of storage media currently supports self encrypting capabilities?
<--- Score

181. What is the relative value of the resource in comparison with others already in the collection?
<--- Score

182. How you are doing at your vulnerabilities?
<--- Score

183. What contributes to a better PCI assessment?
<--- Score

184. Do you restrict physical access to information assets and functions by users and support personnel?
<--- Score

185. How much time between a new threat and a

scan?
<--- Score

186. Do you make operating systems reliable and secure?
<--- Score

187. What is cross-site scripting (xss)?
<--- Score

188. Do you empower single individual to be as a critical part of secure programming?
<--- Score

189. Are you able to check the accuracy of the information?
<--- Score

190. Which is a purpose of a security audit?
<--- Score

191. What is the basic design of the application?
<--- Score

192. What vulnerabilities have been detected in your products?
<--- Score

193. Is human factor common in safety and security?
<--- Score

194. Is the information on it unique?
<--- Score

195. What approaches do you have today for

handling buffer and format string vulnerabilities?
<--- Score

196. Will the cloud vendor remain in business for the next few years?
<--- Score

197. Are personnel trained and provided with awareness programs at least once a year?
<--- Score

198. What is your approach to end user support service delivery?
<--- Score

199. Who will have access to the product?
<--- Score

200. When was the security push, and how long did it take?
<--- Score

201. Can it be forced to give up information?
<--- Score

202. What and where are the common vulnerabilities and why?
<--- Score

203. What would an attacker hope to achieve?
<--- Score

204. Do you logically and physically segregate production and non production environments?
<--- Score

205. Is the logged information consistent and complete?
<--- Score

206. What is your approach to managing the security posture of the IT infrastructure?
<--- Score

207. Is there a limit on the number of times you may test an app?
<--- Score

208. Is the code reviewer knowledgeable about the domain knowledge of the code that is being reviewed?
<--- Score

209. How much uptime is the system providing?
<--- Score

210. Are the connections to it providing the information reliable and stable?
<--- Score

211. Does the information overlap with items already in the collection does it duplicate?
<--- Score

212. Is there an option for multimedia browsers/ line mode browsers?
<--- Score

213. Do you conduct network layer vulnerability scans regularly as prescribed by industry best practices?
<--- Score

214. Do you ensure your providers adhere to your information security and privacy policies?
<--- Score

215. How severe are the vulnerabilities?
<--- Score

216. Is it more efficient than other tools in the literature?
<--- Score

217. Does application support password expiration?
<--- Score

218. Are users made aware of responsibilities for maintaining a safe and secure working environment?
<--- Score

219. Do you fall under FISMA or PCI DSS?
<--- Score

220. Does it lead visitors through the information nicely?
<--- Score

221. How is application security different from network security?
<--- Score

222. What are the consequences of poor cryptographic practices in mobile applications?
<--- Score

223. Is the system going to be physically isolated in a bunker with guards?
<--- Score

224. Are you testing at the unit, subsystem, system of system level?
<--- Score

225. How secure is the credential store access?
<--- Score

226. Is the information accurate, comprehensive?
<--- Score

227. How often do you scan the systems?
<--- Score

228. Who will have visibility into the defect repository?
<--- Score

229. Does the application have a remember you feature?
<--- Score

230. What vulnerability types occur most frequently in your code?
<--- Score

231. How do you make changes to your application when it should be always available?
<--- Score

232. Are you and your organization ready to deal with a cyber crisis?
<--- Score

233. Do you use any technologies to enhance the security posture of your applications?
<--- Score

234. Does your organization regularly compare your security spend with other organizations?
<--- Score

235. Can other local users on the system read, modify or delete files used by the web application?
<--- Score

236. Where is the source code located?
<--- Score

237. How important is the system to the user organizations mission?
<--- Score

238. How does a product get certified?
<--- Score

239. Which are main characteristics of an effective security test environment?
<--- Score

240. Does your application have user mode and kernel mode components?
<--- Score

241. Have you followed security design principles?
<--- Score

242. Is it possible to access that resource after the log out?

<--- Score

243. What are the known regulations or directives from headquarters that will exert influence on how security should be applied to software within your organizations?
<--- Score

244. What makes app security so hard?
<--- Score

245. Why is hardware based encryption more secure than software encryption?
<--- Score

246. How does eside influence the students awareness and mindset of security?
<--- Score

247. Do most projects perform penetration tests prior to release?
<--- Score

248. Are security defaults operating as intended?
<--- Score

249. How did you request the product or service?
<--- Score

250. Do you test your backup or redundancy mechanisms at least annually?
<--- Score

251. Why make an attackers job easier?
<--- Score

252. Is the information from a reputable source?
<--- Score

253. Which vulnerabilities are exploited?
<--- Score

254. Do you have a security architecture?
<--- Score

255. Why are authentication vulnerabilities so dangerous?
<--- Score

256. Does the tool detect the vulnerabilities that it was programmed to detect?
<--- Score

257. Are your top people leaving you and your organization?
<--- Score

258. What is breadth of device support software, network, security?
<--- Score

259. How would you be informed were there an incident or breach that could potentially expose sensitive user information?
<--- Score

260. What xerox software options are available for xerox remote print services?
<--- Score

261. How does a workforce introduce the security skills to implement a secure code review

methodology?
<--- Score

262. Is the information presented accurately?
<--- Score

263. What types of security defects can be detected?
<--- Score

264. What information is being given?
<--- Score

265. Is there a software security assurance program already in place?
<--- Score

266. What is already in the collection?
<--- Score

267. Is the date given stating when the web item was created?
<--- Score

268. Does the application have a keep alive or log you on automatically function?
<--- Score

269. Where do software security assurance tools add value?
<--- Score

270. What is the most effective way to ensure secure application?
<--- Score

271. Will the application know if its being attacked?
<--- Score

272. How do HTML5 technologies should be used securely?
<--- Score

273. Is feature accessible to anonymous users?
<--- Score

274. How do you select a programming language for a project?
<--- Score

275. How easy is it for a potential attack to work?
<--- Score

276. Is the information broken down into digestible parts?
<--- Score

277. Why include tests in a revision?
<--- Score

278. Is it easy to switch the private keys of the system?
<--- Score

279. How effectively can information be retrieved from the resource?
<--- Score

280. What do systems users have to fear?
<--- Score

281. What types of builds are allowed, and where are the images stored?
<--- Score

282. Is the clouds dynamic nature adequately reflected in the logged information?
<--- Score

283. Are your customers satisfied with the products security?
<--- Score

284. Do most projects check for security updates to thirdparty software components?
<--- Score

285. Is the information arranged logically?
<--- Score

286. What are reliability and performance efficiency industry best practices?
<--- Score

287. How many servers are affected if the threat were realized?
<--- Score

288. What are the common programming challenges?
<--- Score

289. What steps do you take to protect your information from unauthorized network access, as malicious internal users, external hackers, viruses, and other types of malware?
<--- Score

290. How critical is security to organizations today?
<--- Score

291. Is a version number for the resource displayed?
<--- Score

292. What testing does your organization perform on your software?
<--- Score

293. How numerous are security flaws compared to security bugs?
<--- Score

294. Which of the application domains best describes your project?
<--- Score

295. Can the administrator perform normal transactions or see the normal application?
<--- Score

296. What defects or vulnerabilities were injected or removed?
<--- Score

297. Is the information durable in nature?
<--- Score

298. Is the code being integrated into the project fully vetted by IT management and approved?
<--- Score

299. Does your organization feel comfortable with outsourcing security testing?
<--- Score

300. Do you run your local desktop as an Administrator user?
<--- Score

301. How do you feel about detecting and mitigating cyber threats in your organization?
<--- Score

302. Does access privilege meet roles?
<--- Score

303. Which code fragment would you choose?
<--- Score

304. What do you see as the main barriers to achieving a strong application security posture?
<--- Score

305. Is the information clearly organized?
<--- Score

306. Is the check at or near the top of the activity?
<--- Score

307. Are time sensitive sources available in near real time?
<--- Score

308. What fraction of the vulnerabilities do you expect to be found by a single security reviewer?
<--- Score

309. Does the application possess remember you functionality?
<--- Score

310. Does the source avoid blink features?
<--- Score

311. What cloud resources does a user have access to?
<--- Score

312. What cloud resources does a user actually access?
<--- Score

313. Where will the workforce mobility revolution take you?
<--- Score

314. What is the breadth of the information?
<--- Score

315. What security properties are supported during software design?
<--- Score

316. Do you provide the tenant the ability to declare a disaster?
<--- Score

317. Is the accuracy of the presentation adequate?
<--- Score

318. Is the information composed well?
<--- Score

319. How often do you do practical programming in your work?
<--- Score

320. Do you access the private keys associated with the signatures?
<--- Score

321. Is it easy to browse the resource?
<--- Score

322. Does organization project estimation allot time for code reviews?
<--- Score

323. Why does string pose a threat to security when it comes to passwords?
<--- Score

324. Is a representation of the security properties supported?
<--- Score

325. Does your feature have any unauthenticated network connections?
<--- Score

326. Can an administrator provision other administrators or just users?
<--- Score

327. What applications are in the cloud?
<--- Score

328. What is your organizations primary means of securing applications?

<--- Score

329. Does it contain breakthrough content or design elements?
<--- Score

330. How will the price evolve over time?
<--- Score

331. Does your code check the referrer?
<--- Score

332. Which information should be logged?
<--- Score

333. What is often considered the weakest link in software security?
<--- Score

334. How open is the application intended to be?
<--- Score

335. Do you know what secure programming / coding is?
<--- Score

336. What is the one thing inherent in all software?
<--- Score

337. Is the information within a resource arranged consistently?
<--- Score

338. Does the application write files with user supplied file names?
<--- Score

339. Can an attacker gain administration access to the system?
<--- Score

340. Is the information what it appears to be?
<--- Score

341. Have an incident management policy?
<--- Score

342. Is your customer information safe?
<--- Score

343. Do you have one million dollars to spend on application security?
<--- Score

344. What it systems do you have in your enterprise?
<--- Score

345. Does the resource contain substantive information?
<--- Score

346. Does the application implement or use any cryptographic mechanisms?
<--- Score

347. How can technologists become forces for the public interest within own organizations?
<--- Score

348. Where are the application properties/ configuration parameters stored?

<--- Score

349. What is your primary role in your organization?
<--- Score

350. Has the information been filtered?
<--- Score

351. Is customer support and training provided?
<--- Score

352. How will management communicate to the other employees?
<--- Score

353. How does vmware help customers achieve reliable business continuity and disaster recovery?
<--- Score

354. Is threat modeling is performed?
<--- Score

355. How are reset passwords communicated to the user?
<--- Score

356. Can an attacker crash the system?
<--- Score

357. Which tools are most effective in detecting security vulnerabilities?
<--- Score

358. Does your application support a null credential or an account with no password?

<--- Score

359. How do you achieve Single Sign-On for your applications?
<--- Score

360. Can an anonymous user retrieve that protected content?
<--- Score

361. How do the tools compare in terms of the severity and number of defects detected?
<--- Score

362. Who could be looking at your information online?
<--- Score

363. Where must an IT team look first?
<--- Score

364. Does the resource follow good design principles?
<--- Score

365. Do you have access to a reusable software library or repository?
<--- Score

366. Is threat modeling or peer reviews being conducted in certain groups?
<--- Score

367. What are the secure design principles that should be applied when designing software?
<--- Score

368. Is there value added information?
<--- Score

369. Does your feature include any script code?
<--- Score

370. Why your web server should offer remote scanning facilities of anyone to anyone?
<--- Score

371. How do you ensure operation of your systems conforms to policy?
<--- Score

372. Does the resource contain more than contact details?
<--- Score

373. Why is information security important?
<--- Score

374. Is the system connected to other systems or networks?
<--- Score

375. Which best describes your role in the IT security function within your organization?
<--- Score

376. Does your organization use one or more Payment Applications?
<--- Score

377. What is the purpose of the resource?
<--- Score

378. Why is an attack from inside your organization particularly worrisome?
<--- Score

379. How does your login experience change?
<--- Score

380. Does the resource point to other sources which could be contacted for confirmation?
<--- Score

381. Is the content amplified over time or is one visit all its worth?
<--- Score

382. Do you conduct application layer vulnerability scans regularly as prescribed by industry best practices?
<--- Score

383. What are the different network interface card options?
<--- Score

384. When is the overall project expected to end?
<--- Score

385. Who is accountable in the networked environment for a vulnerability in an operating system?
<--- Score

386. What category best describes the project relationship with the project customer?
<--- Score

387. How does memory management affect security?
<--- Score

388. What happens to the entropy level in a working linux server under average load?
<--- Score

389. What is available outside the collection?
<--- Score

390. How do you integrate with other identity providers?
<--- Score

391. What networks and systems are included?
<--- Score

392. What weaknesses in your software could be exploited?
<--- Score

393. Does the self registration feature allow full access to all features without human intervention?
<--- Score

394. Do you use secure by design design method in your work?
<--- Score

395. How do you check the authenticity of a website?
<--- Score

396. Do you really bolt on security after the fact?

<--- Score

397. Which assets are valuable to your organization?
<--- Score

398. Does the firewall encrypt all non console administrative access?
<--- Score

399. Is it easy to navigate the resource?
<--- Score

400. Is source code available for the tool?
<--- Score

401. What are the common security vulnerabilities?
<--- Score

402. Does the application rely on client side validation?
<--- Score

403. Are most stakeholders aware of the security test status prior to release?
<--- Score

404. Are the sources of the information stated?
<--- Score

405. How do you configure your systems more securely?
<--- Score

406. How extreme does extreme programming

have to be?
<--- Score

407. Which software security best practices are you familiar with?
<--- Score

408. How important is the information to the user organizations mission?
<--- Score

409. What can be done to reduce defects in software, and thus reduce vulnerabilities in software?
<--- Score

410. How valid is the content of the information?
<--- Score

411. Are any business critical systems on cloud?
<--- Score

412. Is the technical performance of the resource acceptable?
<--- Score

413. How do you know if the CISOs security program has accounted for all the components to be effective?
<--- Score

414. Does production code contain debug error handlers or messages?
<--- Score

415. Which virus types changes its characteristics

as it spreads?
<--- Score

416. What are the secure input validation strategies and how strategies should be implemented?
<--- Score

417. Do you pay bills using an auto pay system?
<--- Score

418. How many users would be affected by the attack?
<--- Score

419. Can the user sign up on line or must written contracts be negotiated first?
<--- Score

420. Does the implementation adopt a modular design with well specified module interfaces?
<--- Score

421. What category best describes the primary product use?
<--- Score

422. Are there stated criteria for inclusion of information?
<--- Score

423. Do you trust code that calls your code?
<--- Score

Add up total points for this section:
_____ = Total points for this section

Divided by: ______ (number of statements answered) = ______ Average score for this section

Transfer your score to the Secure coding Index at the beginning of the Self-Assessment.

Secure coding and Managing Projects, Criteria for Project Managers:

1.0 Initiating Process Group: Secure coding

1. How well did you do?

2. What are the required resources?

3. How will it affect me?

4. Contingency planning. if a risk event occurs, what will you do?

5. Do you understand the quality and control criteria that must be achieved for successful Secure coding project completion?

6. Did the Secure coding project team have the right skills?

7. Does the Secure coding project team have enough people to execute the Secure coding project plan?

8. How well did the chosen processes fit the needs of the Secure coding project?

9. The process to Manage Stakeholders is part of which process group?

10. When will the Secure coding project be done?

11. Were decisions made in a timely manner?

12. How to control and approve each phase?

13. What do they need to know about the Secure

coding project?

14. Are identified risks being monitored properly, are new risks arising during the Secure coding project or are foreseen risks occurring?

15. What areas were overlooked on this Secure coding project?

16. Who is funding the Secure coding project?

17. Do you understand the communication expectations for this Secure coding project?

18. At which cmmi level are software processes documented, standardized, and integrated into a standard to-be practiced process for your organization?

19. During which stage of Risk planning are modeling techniques used to determine overall effects of risks on Secure coding project objectives for high probability, high impact risks?

20. Are there resources to maintain and support the outcome of the Secure coding project?

1.1 Project Charter: Secure coding

21. Major high-level milestone targets: what events measure progress?

22. How much?

23. Are you building in-house ?

24. Success determination factors: how will the success of the Secure coding project be determined from the customers perspective?

25. What are some examples of a business case?

26. How will you learn more about the process or system you are trying to improve?

27. How will you know a change is an improvement?

28. Name and describe the elements that deal with providing the detail?

29. What changes can you make to improve?

30. What outcome, in measureable terms, are you hoping to accomplish?

31. Who are the stakeholders?

32. What barriers do you predict to your success?

33. Assumptions and constraints: what assumptions were made in defining the Secure coding project?

34. When do you use a Secure coding project Charter?

35. Will this replace an existing product?

36. What ideas do you have for initial tests of change (PDSA cycles)?

37. What does it need to do?

38. Fit with other Products Compliments – Cannibalizes?

39. Where and how does the team fit within your organization structure?

40. When?

1.2 Stakeholder Register: Secure coding

41. What & Why?

42. Who wants to talk about Security?

43. How will reports be created?

44. How big is the gap?

45. What is the power of the stakeholder?

46. How should employers make voices heard?

47. Who is managing stakeholder engagement?

48. Is your organization ready for change?

49. What opportunities exist to provide communications?

50. What are the major Secure coding project milestones requiring communications or providing communications opportunities?

51. How much influence do they have on the Secure coding project?

1.3 Stakeholder Analysis Matrix: Secure coding

52. Resources, assets, people?

53. Financial reserves, likely returns?

54. What resources might the stakeholder bring to the Secure coding project?

55. Are they likely to influence the success or failure of your Secure coding project?

56. Volumes, production, economies?

57. Does the stakeholder want to be involved or merely need to be informed about the Secure coding project and its process?

58. Who will be affected by the Secure coding project?

59. Gaps in capabilities?

60. Are there different rules or organizational models for men and women?

61. What are the opportunities for communication?

62. What unique or lowest-cost resources does the Secure coding project have access to?

63. Arena: in what fields are the actors active, where are they present?

64. What could your organization improve?

65. Supporters; who are the supporters?

66. What is the stakeholders mandate, what is mission?

67. Which conditions out of the control of the management are crucial for the achievement of the outputs?

68. Which conditions out of the control of the management are crucial for the achievement of the immediate objective?

69. What is in it for you?

70. Do recommendations include actions to address any differential distribution of impacts?

71. Are there people who ise voices or interests in the issue may not be heard?

2.0 Planning Process Group: Secure coding

72. On which process should team members spend the most time?

73. Are the follow-up indicators relevant and do they meet the quality needed to measure the outputs and outcomes of the Secure coding project?

74. What will you do to minimize the impact should a risk event occur?

75. How will you know you did it?

76. What should you do next?

77. How do you integrate Secure coding project Planning with the Iterative/Evolutionary SDLC?

78. How can you make your needs known?

79. Is your organization showing technical capacity and leadership commitment to keep working with the Secure coding project and to repeat it?

80. What input will you be required to provide the Secure coding project team?

81. First of all, should any action be taken?

82. If a risk event occurs, what will you do?

83. Will the products created live up to the necessary quality?

84. To what extent do the intervention objectives and strategies of the Secure coding project respond to your organizations plans?

85. Just how important is your work to the overall success of the Secure coding project?

86. Explanation: is what the Secure coding project intents to solve a hard question?

87. What good practices or successful experiences or transferable examples have been identified?

88. Do the partners have sufficient financial capacity to keep up the benefits produced by the programme?

89. What factors are contributing to progress or delay in the achievement of products and results?

90. What do they need to know about the Secure coding project?

91. What types of differentiated effects are resulting from the Secure coding project and to what extent?

2.1 Project Management Plan: Secure coding

92. What are the assumptions?

93. What goes into your Secure coding project Charter?

94. What are the training needs?

95. Does the implementation plan have an appropriate division of responsibilities?

96. What are the known stakeholder requirements?

97. Does the selected plan protect privacy?

98. What would you do differently what did not work?

99. Do the proposed changes from the Secure coding project include any significant risks to safety?

100. What did not work so well?

101. Are there any client staffing expectations?

102. What if, for example, the positive direction and vision of your organization causes expected trends to change resulting in greater need than expected?

103. Will you add a schedule and diagram?

104. Are cost risk analysis methods applied to develop

contingencies for the estimated total Secure coding project costs?

105. If the Secure coding project management plan is a comprehensive document that guides you in Secure coding project execution and control, then what should it NOT contain?

106. What are the constraints?

107. What would you do differently?

108. What went wrong?

109. When is the Secure coding project management plan created?

110. How well are you able to manage your risk?

111. Is mitigation authorized or recommended?

2.2 Scope Management Plan: Secure coding

112. Will your organizations estimating methodology be used and followed?

113. Have all documents been archived in a Secure coding project repository for each release?

114. Have activity relationships and interdependencies within tasks been adequately identified?

115. What are the risks that could significantly affect the schedule of the Secure coding project?

116. Are you spending the right amount of money for specific tasks?

117. Are internal Secure coding project status meetings held at reasonable intervals?

118. During what part of the PM process is the Secure coding project scope statement created?

119. Are risk oriented checklists used during risk identification?

120. Are trade-offs between accepting the risk and mitigating the risk identified?

121. Has your organization readiness assessment been conducted?

122. Are corrective actions and variances reported?

123. Are target dates established for each milestone deliverable?

124. Pareto diagrams, statistical sampling, flow charting or trend analysis used quality monitoring?

125. Is pert / critical path or equivalent methodology being used?

126. Have all unresolved risks been documented?

127. Timeline and milestones?

128. Has the business need been clearly defined?

129. Have external dependencies been captured in the schedule?

130. To whom will the deliverables be first presented for inspection and verification?

2.3 Requirements Management Plan: Secure coding

131. Is requirements work dependent on any other specific Secure coding project or non-Secure coding project activities (e.g. funding, approvals, procurement)?

132. To see if a requirement statement is sufficiently well-defined, read it from the developers perspective. Mentally add the phrase, call me when youre done to the end of the requirement and see if that makes you nervous. In other words, would you need additional clarification from the author to understand the requirement well enough to design and implement it?

133. Who came up with this requirement?

134. What are you counting on?

135. Who will approve the requirements (and if multiple approvers, in what order)?

136. Do you have an agreed upon process for alerting the Secure coding project Manager if a request for change in requirements leads to a product scope change?

137. Define the help desk model. who will take full responsibility?

138. Is the system software (non-operating system) new to the IT Secure coding project team?

139. When and how will a requirements baseline be established in this Secure coding project?

140. Will the contractors involved take full responsibility?

141. Did you get proper approvals?

142. What is the earliest finish date for this Secure coding project if it is scheduled to start on ...?

143. Is it new or replacing an existing business system or process?

144. Could inaccurate or incomplete requirements in this Secure coding project create a serious risk for the business?

145. Did you distinguish the scope of work the contractor(s) will be required to do?

146. After the requirements are gathered and set forth on the requirements register, theyre little more than a laundry list of items. Some may be duplicates, some might conflict with others and some will be too broad or too vague to understand. Describe how the requirements will be analyzed. Who will perform the analysis?

147. Do you know which stakeholders will participate in the requirements effort?

148. Who will initially review the Secure coding project work or products to ensure it meets the applicable acceptance criteria?

149. In case of software development; Should you have a test for each code module?

2.4 Requirements Documentation: Secure coding

150. How do you know when a Requirement is accurate enough?

151. Are there legal issues?

152. What are current process problems?

153. Can the requirements be checked?

154. Where are business rules being captured?

155. What if the system wasn t implemented?

156. What variations exist for a process?

157. Consistency. are there any requirements conflicts?

158. Who provides requirements?

159. Is the origin of the requirement clearly stated?

160. What kind of entity is a problem ?

161. What images does it conjure?

162. Have the benefits identified with the system being identified clearly?

163. Completeness. are all functions required by the

customer included?

164. Is the requirement realistically testable?

165. What is your Elevator Speech?

166. What are the acceptance criteria?

167. What is the risk associated with cost and schedule?

168. Has requirements gathering uncovered information that would necessitate changes?

169. How will they be documented / shared?

2.5 Requirements Traceability Matrix: Secure coding

170. How will it affect the stakeholders personally in career?

171. What percentage of Secure coding projects are producing traceability matrices between requirements and other work products?

172. Do you have a clear understanding of all subcontracts in place?

173. Describe the process for approving requirements so they can be added to the traceability matrix and Secure coding project work can be performed. Will the Secure coding project requirements become approved in writing?

174. How small is small enough?

175. Is there a requirements traceability process in place?

176. Why do you manage scope?

177. How do you manage scope?

178. Why use a WBS?

179. What are the chronologies, contingencies, consequences, criteria?

180. Will you use a Requirements Traceability Matrix?

181. What is the WBS?

2.6 Project Scope Statement: Secure coding

182. What are the possible consequences should a risk come to occur?

183. Is the quality function identified and assigned?

184. Is an issue management process documented and filed?

185. Is there a baseline plan against which to measure progress?

186. Change management vs. change leadership - what is the difference?

187. Is there an information system for the Secure coding project?

188. What actions will be taken to mitigate the risk?

189. Are there completion/verification criteria defined for each task producing an output?

190. Was planning completed before the Secure coding project was initiated?

191. What is the most common tool for helping define the detail?

192. What process would you recommend for creating the Secure coding project scope statement?

193. Has the format for tracking and monitoring schedules and costs been defined?

194. Is there a process (test plans, inspections, reviews) defined for verifying outputs for each task?

195. What is the product of this Secure coding project?

196. Identify how your team and you will create the Secure coding project scope statement and the work breakdown structure (WBS). Document how you will create the Secure coding project scope statement and WBS, and make sure you answer the following questions: In defining Secure coding project scope and the WBS, will you and your Secure coding project team be using methods defined by your organization, methods defined by the Secure coding project management office (PMO), or other methods?

197. Is there a Quality Assurance Plan documented and filed?

198. What should you drop in order to add something new?

199. Do you anticipate new stakeholders joining the Secure coding project over time?

200. Will the Secure coding project risks be managed according to the Secure coding projects risk management process?

201. Were key Secure coding project stakeholders brought into the Secure coding project Plan?

2.7 Assumption and Constraint Log: Secure coding

202. Are funding and staffing resource estimates sufficiently detailed and documented for use in planning and tracking the Secure coding project?

203. Was the document/deliverable developed per the appropriate or required standards (for example, Institute of Electrical and Electronics Engineers standards)?

204. After observing execution of process, is it in compliance with the documented Plan?

205. What do you log?

206. Does a specific action and/or state that is known to violate security policy occur?

207. Have adequate resources been provided by management to ensure Secure coding project success?

208. Does the document/deliverable meet all requirements (for example, statement of work) specific to this deliverable?

209. What other teams / processes would be impacted by changes to the current process, and how?

210. Does a documented Secure coding project organizational policy & plan (i.e. governance model)

exist?

211. Is there adequate stakeholder participation for the vetting of requirements definition, changes and management?

212. Have Secure coding project management standards and procedures been established and documented?

213. What worked well?

214. When can log be discarded?

215. Can you perform this task or activity in a more effective manner?

216. Is the steering committee active in Secure coding project oversight?

217. How relevant is this attribute to this Secure coding project or audit?

218. What weaknesses do you have?

219. No superfluous information or marketing narrative?

220. How can constraints be violated?

221. Have the scope, objectives, costs, benefits and impacts been communicated to all involved and/or impacted stakeholders and work groups?

2.8 Work Breakdown Structure: Secure coding

222. What is the probability of completing the Secure coding project in less that xx days?

223. Is the work breakdown structure (wbs) defined and is the scope of the Secure coding project clear with assigned deliverable owners?

224. How will you and your Secure coding project team define the Secure coding projects scope and work breakdown structure?

225. What is the probability that the Secure coding project duration will exceed xx weeks?

226. When would you develop a Work Breakdown Structure?

227. How much detail?

228. Can you make it?

229. Why would you develop a Work Breakdown Structure?

230. When do you stop?

231. Where does it take place?

232. Who has to do it?

233. Is it still viable?

234. Do you need another level?

235. Is it a change in scope?

236. How far down?

237. When does it have to be done?

238. Why is it useful?

239. What has to be done?

2.9 WBS Dictionary: Secure coding

240. Budgeted cost for work performed?

241. Are work packages assigned to performing organizations?

242. Appropriate work authorization documents which subdivide the contractual effort and responsibilities, within functional organizations?

243. Detailed schedules which support control account and work package start and completion dates/events?

244. Contractor financial periods; for example, annual?

245. Is work progressively subdivided into detailed work packages as requirements are defined?

246. Knowledgeable Secure coding projections of future performance?

247. Are records maintained to show full accountability for all material purchased for the contract, including the residual inventory?

248. Should you include sub-activities?

249. Are estimates of costs at completion utilized in determining contract funding requirements and reporting them?

250. What is the goal?

251. Are estimates developed by Secure coding project personnel coordinated with the already stated responsible for overall management to determine whether required resources will be available according to revised planning?

252. Are the requirements for all items of overhead established by rational, traceable processes?

253. Is all contract work included in the CWBS?

254. Are all affected work authorizations, budgeting, and scheduling documents amended to properly reflect the effects of authorized changes?

255. The wbs is developed as part of a joint planning session. and how do you know that youhave done this right?

256. The Secure coding projected business base for each period?

257. Are the contractors estimates of costs at completion reconcilable with cost data reported to us?

258. Are the variances between budgeted and actual indirect costs identified and analyzed at the level of assigned responsibility for control (indirect pool, department, etc.)?

2.10 Schedule Management Plan: Secure coding

259. After initial schedule development, will the schedule be reviewed and validated by the Secure coding project team?

260. Are the constraints or deadlines associated with the task accurate?

261. Will the Secure coding project sponsor be involved in preliminary schedule reviews?

262. Does the business case include how the Secure coding project aligns with your organizations strategic goals & objectives?

263. Is the quality assurance team identified?

264. Is the schedule vertically and horizontally traceable?

265. Have the key elements of a coherent Secure coding project management strategy been established?

266. Are the Secure coding project team members located locally to the users/stakeholders?

267. Have the key functions and capabilities been defined and assigned to each release or iteration?

268. Have key stakeholders been identified?

269. Are all vendor contracts closed out?

270. Are changes in deliverable commitments agreed to by all affected groups & individuals?

271. Is the plan consistent with industry best practices?

272. Is there anything planned that does not need to be here?

273. What tools and techniques will be used to estimate activity durations?

274. Are the quality tools and methods identified in the Quality Plan appropriate to the Secure coding project?

275. Were stakeholders aware and supportive of the principles and practices of modern software estimation?

276. Is the assigned Secure coding project manager a PMP (Certified Secure coding project manager) and experienced?

277. Is funded schedule margin reasonable and logically distributed?

2.11 Activity List: Secure coding

278. What are the critical bottleneck activities?

279. How detailed should a Secure coding project get?

280. What went well?

281. What is the LF and LS for each activity?

282. How much slack is available in the Secure coding project?

283. How difficult will it be to do specific activities on this Secure coding project?

284. How do you determine the late start (LS) for each activity?

285. When do the individual activities need to start and finish?

286. What will be performed?

287. Can you determine the activity that must finish, before this activity can start?

288. What went right?

289. For other activities, how much delay can be tolerated?

290. In what sequence?

291. How should ongoing costs be monitored to try to keep the Secure coding project within budget?

292. What is your organizations history in doing similar activities?

293. How can the Secure coding project be displayed graphically to better visualize the activities?

294. Where will it be performed?

2.12 Activity Attributes: Secure coding

295. How difficult will it be to do specific activities on this Secure coding project?

296. Activity: fair or not fair?

297. Can more resources be added?

298. Have you identified the Activity Leveling Priority code value on each activity?

299. How much activity detail is required?

300. Why?

301. Can you re-assign any activities to another resource to resolve an over-allocation?

302. Were there other ways you could have organized the data to achieve similar results?

303. Are the required resources available?

304. How else could the items be grouped?

305. Activity: what is In the Bag?

306. Activity: what is Missing?

307. What is missing?

308. How many days do you need to complete the work scope with a limit of X number of resources?

309. How many resources do you need to complete the work scope within a limit of X number of days?

310. What conclusions/generalizations can you draw from this?

2.13 Milestone List: Secure coding

311. What has been done so far?

312. Continuity, supply chain robustness?

313. How will you get the word out to customers?

314. Reliability of data, plan predictability?

315. How will the milestone be verified?

316. Political effects?

317. How late can the activity start?

318. Identify critical paths (one or more) and which activities are on the critical path?

319. Level of the Innovation?

320. Sustaining internal capabilities?

321. Effects on core activities, distraction?

322. Marketing - reach, distribution, awareness?

323. Insurmountable weaknesses?

324. Global influences?

325. What is the market for your technology, product or service?

326. Vital contracts and partners?

327. Describe the concept of the technology, product or service that will be or has been developed. How will it be used?

328. When will the Secure coding project be complete?

329. What background experience, skills, and strengths does the team bring to your organization?

330. How late can each activity be finished and started?

2.14 Network Diagram: Secure coding

331. What activity must be completed immediately before this activity can start?

332. Why must you schedule milestones, such as reviews, throughout the Secure coding project?

333. What are the Major Administrative Issues?

334. If x is long, what would be the completion time if you break x into two parallel parts of y weeks and z weeks?

335. What to do and When?

336. Will crashing x weeks return more in benefits than it costs?

337. Can you calculate the confidence level?

338. Where do you schedule uncertainty time?

339. What job or jobs follow it?

340. If the Secure coding project network diagram cannot change and you have extra personnel resources, what is the BEST thing to do?

341. What job or jobs could run concurrently?

342. Planning: who, how long, what to do?

343. What activities must occur simultaneously with

this activity?

344. What controls the start and finish of a job?

345. What is the completion time?

346. Are the gantt chart and/or network diagram updated periodically and used to assess the overall Secure coding project timetable?

347. What are the tools?

348. Review the logical flow of the network diagram. Take a look at which activities you have first and then sequence the activities. Do they make sense?

349. How difficult will it be to do specific activities on this Secure coding project?

2.15 Activity Resource Requirements: Secure coding

350. What are constraints that you might find during the Human Resource Planning process?

351. What is the Work Plan Standard?

352. Other support in specific areas?

353. Do you use tools like decomposition and rolling-wave planning to produce the activity list and other outputs?

354. Which logical relationship does the PDM use most often?

355. When does monitoring begin?

356. How do you handle petty cash?

357. Anything else?

358. How many signatures do you require on a check and does this match what is in your policy and procedures?

359. How do you manage time?

360. Organizational Applicability?

361. Why do you do that?

362. Time for overtime?

363. Are there unresolved issues that need to be addressed?

2.16 Resource Breakdown Structure: Secure coding

364. What defines a successful Secure coding project?

365. Who delivers the information?

366. How should the information be delivered?

367. What is the purpose of assigning and documenting responsibility?

368. What is the primary purpose of the human resource plan?

369. Who will use the system?

370. Changes based on input from stakeholders?

371. What is Secure coding project communication management?

372. Goals for the Secure coding project. What is each stakeholders desired outcome for the Secure coding project?

373. Which resource planning tool provides information on resource responsibility and accountability?

374. Why do you do it?

375. Any changes from stakeholders?

376. What is each stakeholders desired outcome for the Secure coding project?

377. Who needs what information?

378. Why time management?

379. The list could probably go on, but, the thing that you would most like to know is, How long & How much?

2.17 Activity Duration Estimates: Secure coding

380. Who will provide training for the new application?

381. Is a Secure coding project charter created once a Secure coding project is formally recognized?

382. How does a Secure coding project life cycle differ from a product life cycle?

383. Are updates on work results collected and used as inputs to the performance reporting process?

384. Based on , if you need to shorten the duration of the Secure coding project, what activity would you try to shorten?

385. How does Secure coding project management relate to other disciplines?

386. If the optimiztic estimate for an activity is 12days, and the pessimistic estimate is 18days, what is the standard deviation of this activity?

387. After changes are approved are Secure coding project documents updated and distributed?

388. How can software assist in procuring goods and services?

389. What do you think about the WBSs for them?

390. Are Secure coding project management tools and techniques consistently applied throughout all Secure coding projects?

391. Sigma Secure coding project?

392. Are contractor costs, schedule and technical performance monitored throughout the Secure coding project?

393. Does a process exist to identify Secure coding project roles, responsibilities and reporting relationships?

394. What are the typical challenges Secure coding project teams face during each of the five process groups?

395. Is a work breakdown structure created to organize and to confirm the scope of each Secure coding project?

396. What are the main processes included in Secure coding project quality management?

397. Briefly describe some key events in the history of Secure coding project management. What Secure coding project was the first to use modern Secure coding project management?

398. Would you rate yourself as being risk-averse, risk-neutral, or risk-seeking?

2.18 Duration Estimating Worksheet: Secure coding

399. What work will be included in the Secure coding project?

400. What is cost and Secure coding project cost management?

401. What is an Average Secure coding project?

402. What utility impacts are there?

403. When, then?

404. Can the Secure coding project be constructed as planned?

405. Why estimate costs?

406. What is your role?

407. What questions do you have?

408. Science = process: remember the scientific method?

409. Will the Secure coding project collaborate with the local community and leverage resources?

410. Define the work as completely as possible. What work will be included in the Secure coding project?

411. Is a construction detail attached (to aid in explanation)?

412. Do any colleagues have experience with your organization and/or RFPs?

413. Done before proceeding with this activity or what can be done concurrently?

2.19 Project Schedule: Secure coding

414. What is Secure coding project management?

415. How do you use schedules?

416. What is the difference?

417. Are key risk mitigation strategies added to the Secure coding project schedule?

418. How can you minimize or control changes to Secure coding project schedules?

419. Why is software Secure coding project disaster so common?

420. Understand the constraints used in preparing the schedule. Are activities connected because logic dictates the order in which others occur?

421. What does that mean?

422. Your best shot for providing estimations how complex/how much work does the activity require?

423. Meet requirements?

424. Did the final product meet or exceed user expectations?

425. Are procedures defined by which the Secure coding project schedule may be changed?

426. How do you manage Secure coding project Risk?

427. If there are any qualifying green components to this Secure coding project, what portion of the total Secure coding project cost is green?

428. Activity charts and bar charts are graphical representations of a Secure coding project schedule ...how do they differ?

429. Does the condition or event threaten the Secure coding projects objectives in any ways?

430. Are the original Secure coding project schedule and budget realistic?

431. How detailed should a Secure coding project get?

2.20 Cost Management Plan: Secure coding

432. Has the scope management document been updated and distributed to help prevent scope creep?

433. Are the results of quality assurance reviews provided to affected groups & individuals?

434. Has a sponsor been identified?

435. Eac -estimate at completion, what is the total job expected to cost?

436. Is Secure coding project work proceeding in accordance with the original Secure coding project schedule?

437. Is there a formal set of procedures supporting Issues Management?

438. Was the Secure coding project schedule reviewed by all stakeholders and formally accepted?

439. Is an industry recognized mechanized support tool(s) being used for Secure coding project scheduling & tracking?

440. Is a pmo (Secure coding project management office) in place and provide oversight to the Secure coding project?

441. Are tasks tracked by hours?

442. Is there any form of automated support for Issues Management?

443. Quality assurance overheads?

444. Contingency – how will cost contingency be administered?

445. Do all stakeholders know how to access this repository and where to find the Secure coding project documentation?

446. Is there anything unique in this Secure coding projects scope statement that will affect resources?

447. Has the Secure coding project scope been baselined?

448. Is there a requirements change management processes in place?

2.21 Activity Cost Estimates: Secure coding

449. Who & what determines the need for contracted services?

450. What is included in indirect cost being allocated?

451. How do you fund change orders?

452. Would you hire them again?

453. Did the consultant work with local staff to develop local capacity?

454. How Award?

455. Will you use any tools, such as Secure coding project management software, to assist in capturing Earned Value metrics?

456. What is the Secure coding projects sustainability strategy that will ensure Secure coding project results will endure or be sustained?

457. What are you looking for?

458. How do you allocate indirect costs to activities?

459. In which phase of the acquisition process cycle does source qualifications reside?

460. What defines a successful Secure coding project?

461. Does the estimator estimate by task or by person?

462. Measurable - are the targets measurable?

463. Does the activity use a common approach or business function to deliver its results?

464. Vac -variance at completion, how much over/ under budget do you expect to be?

465. What areas were overlooked on this Secure coding project?

466. What is Secure coding project cost management?

2.22 Cost Estimating Worksheet: Secure coding

467. Who is best positioned to know and assist in identifying corresponding factors?

468. What info is needed?

469. Identify the timeframe necessary to monitor progress and collect data to determine how the selected measure has changed?

470. What can be included?

471. What is the estimated labor cost today based upon this information?

472. Value pocket identification & quantification what are value pockets?

473. What will others want?

474. Ask: are others positioned to know, are others credible, and will others cooperate?

475. Is the Secure coding project responsive to community need?

476. Will the Secure coding project collaborate with the local community and leverage resources?

477. What costs are to be estimated?

478. Does the Secure coding project provide innovative ways for stakeholders to overcome obstacles or deliver better outcomes?

479. What is the purpose of estimating?

480. Can a trend be established from historical performance data on the selected measure and are the criteria for using trend analysis or forecasting methods met?

481. What happens to any remaining funds not used?

482. What additional Secure coding project(s) could be initiated as a result of this Secure coding project?

483. How will the results be shared and to whom?

484. Is it feasible to establish a control group arrangement?

2.23 Cost Baseline: Secure coding

485. On time?

486. Should a more thorough impact analysis be conducted?

487. Review your risk triggers -have your risks changed?

488. Is there anything unique in this Secure coding projects scope statement that will affect resources?

489. If you sold 10x widgets on a day, what would the affect on profits be?

490. Are procedures defined by which the cost baseline may be changed?

491. Does the suggested change request seem to represent a necessary enhancement to the product?

492. Does a process exist for establishing a cost baseline to measure Secure coding project performance?

493. Has the Secure coding projected annual cost to operate and maintain the product(s) or service(s) been approved and funded?

494. What strengths do you have?

495. Has the appropriate access to relevant data and analysis capability been granted?

496. What does a good WBS NOT look like?

497. What threats might prevent you from getting there?

498. Is the cr within Secure coding project scope?

499. Definition of done can be traced back to the definitions of what are you providing to the customer in terms of deliverables?

500. How do you manage cost?

501. Have all approved changes to the schedule baseline been identified and impact on the Secure coding project documented?

2.24 Quality Management Plan: Secure coding

502. How are data handled when a test is not run per specification?

503. What changes can you make that will result in improvement?

504. How do you field-modify testing procedures?

505. Documented results available?

506. Show/provide copy of procedures for taking field notes?

507. Who gets results of work?

508. Was trending evident between reviews?

509. What is quality and how will you ensure it?

510. How do you document and correct nonconformances?

511. What is your organizations strategic planning process?

512. What is the Quality Management Plan?

513. Contradictory information between document sections?

514. Are formal code reviews conducted?

515. Have all involved stakeholders and work groups committed to the Secure coding project?

516. How does your organization perform analyzes to assess overall organizational performance and set priorities?

517. How does your organization determine the requirements and product/service features important to customers?

518. What are your organizations current levels and trends for the already stated measures related to financial and marketplace performance?

519. How do you check in-coming sample material?

520. How are people conducting sampling trained?

521. Is there a Quality Management Plan?

2.25 Quality Metrics: Secure coding

522. What is the timeline to meet your goal?

523. What about still open problems?

524. Are quality metrics defined?

525. What is the benchmark?

526. Were quality attributes reported?

527. What does this tell us?

528. How does one achieve stability?

529. What method of measurement do you use?

530. Does risk analysis documentation meet standards?

531. How do you know if everyone is trying to improve the right things?

532. Is quality culture a competitive advantage?

533. Can you correlate your quality metrics to profitability?

534. Should a modifier be included?

535. Which report did you use to create the data you are submitting?

536. When will the Final Guidance will be issued?

537. Are documents on hand to provide explanations of privacy and confidentiality?

538. When is the security analysis testing complete?

539. Are applicable standards referenced and available?

540. Have alternatives been defined in the event that failure occurs?

2.26 Process Improvement Plan: Secure coding

541. What is the return on investment?

542. Have the supporting tools been developed or acquired?

543. Are you following the quality standards?

544. Are you making progress on the improvement framework?

545. How do you manage quality?

546. Why quality management?

547. Have the frequency of collection and the points in the process where measurements will be made been determined?

548. Does your process ensure quality?

549. Where do you focus?

550. Has the time line required to move measurement results from the points of collection to databases or users been established?

551. What is the test-cycle concept?

552. Where are you now?

553. Are you meeting the quality standards?

554. What makes people good SPI coaches?

555. Are there forms and procedures to collect and record the data?

556. To elicit goal statements, do you ask a question such as, What do you want to achieve?

557. Does explicit definition of the measures exist?

558. Who should prepare the process improvement action plan?

559. If a process improvement framework is being used, which elements will help the problems and goals listed?

2.27 Responsibility Assignment Matrix: Secure coding

560. Do others have the time to dedicate to your Secure coding project?

561. Does the scheduling system identify in a timely manner the status of work?

562. What will the work cost?

563. If a role has only Signing-off, or only Communicating responsibility and has no Performing, Accountable, or Monitoring responsibility, is it necessary?

564. Identify potential or actual budget-based and time-based schedule variances?

565. The anticipated business volume?

566. What do you do when people do not respond?

567. Is the anticipated (firm and potential) business base Secure coding projected in a rational, consistent manner?

568. Are indirect costs accumulated for comparison with the corresponding budgets?

569. What expertise is available in your department?

570. Too many as: does a proper segregation of duties

exist?

571. Identify and isolate causes of favorable and unfavorable cost and schedule variances?

572. What is the business need?

573. Are data elements reconcilable between internal summary reports and reports forwarded to stakeholders?

574. Are there any drawbacks to using a responsibility assignment matrix?

575. What expertise is not available in your department?

576. Are people encouraged to bring up issues?

2.28 Roles and Responsibilities: Secure coding

577. What should you do now to ensure that you are meeting all expectations of your current position?

578. Is there a training program in place for stakeholders covering expectations, roles and responsibilities and any addition knowledge others need to be good stakeholders?

579. Are Secure coding project team roles and responsibilities identified and documented?

580. Are your budgets supportive of a culture of quality data?

581. Do the values and practices inherent in the culture of your organization foster or hinder the process?

582. Who is responsible for each task?

583. What expectations were met?

584. Is feedback clearly communicated and non-judgmental?

585. Be specific; avoid generalities. Thank you and great work alone are insufficient. What exactly do you appreciate and why?

586. Once the responsibilities are defined for the

Secure coding project, have the deliverables, roles and responsibilities been clearly communicated to every participant?

587. Influence: what areas of organizational decision making are you able to influence when you do not have authority to make the final decision?

588. Was the expectation clearly communicated?

589. Required skills, knowledge, experience?

590. Have you ever been a part of this team?

591. Does your vision/mission support a culture of quality data?

592. What specific behaviors did you observe?

593. Authority: what areas/Secure coding projects in your work do you have the authority to decide upon and act on the already stated decisions?

594. Key conclusions and recommendations: Are conclusions and recommendations relevant and acceptable?

595. Who: who is involved?

596. Who is involved?

2.29 Human Resource Management Plan: Secure coding

597. Are adequate resources provided for the quality assurance function?

598. Is a stakeholder management plan in place that covers topics?

599. What areas were overlooked on this Secure coding project?

600. Identify who is needed on the core Secure coding project team to complete Secure coding project deliverables and achieve its goals and objectives. What skills, knowledge and experiences are required?

601. Are risk triggers captured?

602. Are vendor contract reports, reviews and visits conducted periodically?

603. What areas does the group agree are the biggest success on the Secure coding project?

604. Are governance roles and responsibilities documented?

605. Does the schedule include Secure coding project management time and change request analysis time?

606. What is this Secure coding project aiming to achieve?

607. How well does your organization communicate?

608. How complete is the human resource management plan?

609. Staffing Requirements?

610. Are multiple estimation methods being employed?

611. What communication items need improvement?

612. Are the appropriate IT resources adequate to meet planned commitments?

613. Does all Secure coding project documentation reside in a common repository for easy access?

614. Has a provision been made to reassess Secure coding project risks at various Secure coding project stages?

615. Are all key components of a Quality Assurance Plan present?

2.30 Communications Management Plan: Secure coding

616. Do you then often overlook a key stakeholder or stakeholder group?

617. Why is stakeholder engagement important?

618. What does the stakeholder need from the team?

619. Who will use or be affected by the result of a Secure coding project?

620. How often do you engage with stakeholders?

621. Do you feel a register helps?

622. What approaches do you use?

623. How much time does it take to do it?

624. Is the stakeholder role recognized by your organization?

625. Who is responsible?

626. Which team member will work with each stakeholder?

627. What to know?

628. Where do team members get information?

629. How will the person responsible for executing the communication item be notified?

630. What is the political influence?

631. Conflict resolution -which method when?

632. In your work, how much time is spent on stakeholder identification?

633. Who is the stakeholder?

634. Will messages be directly related to the release strategy or phases of the Secure coding project?

2.31 Risk Management Plan: Secure coding

635. How quickly does each item need to be resolved?

636. Are enough people available?

637. Is the customer willing to establish rapid communication links with the developer?

638. How is risk identification performed?

639. Do the people have the right combinations of skills?

640. Do you have a consistent repeatable process that is actually used?

641. User involvement: do you have the right users?

642. Are you on schedule?

643. Workarounds are determined during which step of risk management?

644. Have customers been involved fully in the definition of requirements?

645. Do end-users have realistic expectations?

646. Are status updates being made on schedule and are the updates clearly described?

647. What does a risk management program do?

648. Number of users of the product?

649. Prioritized components/features?

650. What is the likelihood that your organization would accept responsibility for the risk?

651. For software; are compilers and code generators available and suitable for the product to be built?

652. How will the Secure coding project know if your organizations risk response actions were effective?

653. Are the reports useful and easy to read?

2.32 Risk Register: Secure coding

654. What are the assumptions and current status that support the assessment of the risk?

655. People risk -are people with appropriate skills available to help complete the Secure coding project?

656. What should you do when?

657. What further options might be available for responding to the risk?

658. Are there other alternative controls that could be implemented?

659. What are the main aims, objectives of the policy, strategy, or service and the intended outcomes?

660. What can be done about it?

661. Who needs to know about this?

662. Methodology: how will risk management be performed on this Secure coding project?

663. Are corrective measures implemented as planned?

664. What are you going to do to limit the Secure coding projects risk exposure due to the identified risks?

665. Severity Prediction?

666. Technology risk -is the Secure coding project technically feasible?

667. Assume the event happens, what is the Most Likely impact?

668. Have other controls and solutions been implemented in other services which could be applied as an alternative to additional funding?

669. Market risk -will the new service or product be useful to your organization or marketable to others?

670. How are risks identified?

671. Do you require further engagement?

672. Having taken action, how did the responses effect change, and where is the Secure coding project now?

673. When is it going to be done?

2.33 Probability and Impact Assessment: Secure coding

674. Which functions, departments, and activities of your organization are going to be affected?

675. What will be cost of redeployment of personnel?

676. Will new information become available during the Secure coding project?

677. What kind of preparation would be required to do this?

678. How do risks change during the Secure coding projects life cycle?

679. Should the risk be taken at all?

680. Who are the international/overseas Secure coding project partners (equipment supplier/ supplier/consultant/contractor) for this Secure coding project?

681. Are Secure coding project requirements stable?

682. Can this technology be absorbed with current level of expertise available in your organization?

683. Can you stabilize dynamic risk factors?

684. What are the chances the risk event will occur?

685. What is the experience (performance, attitude, business ethics, etc.) in the past with contractors?

686. Are the risk data complete?

687. Do you have specific methods that you use for each phase of the process?

688. Have decisions that should be left open because of inadequate information on technology been identified and responsibility assigned for reducing the uncertainty?

689. Do the requirements require the creation of new algorithms?

690. Is the customer technically sophisticated in the product area?

691. Is it necessary to deeply assess all Secure coding project risks?

692. Are tool mentors available?

693. What are the probabilities of chosen technologies being suitable for local conditions?

2.34 Probability and Impact Matrix: Secure coding

694. What are the chances the event will occur?

695. Are flexibility and reuse paramount?

696. Pay attention to the quality of the plans: is the content complete, or does it seem to be lacking detail?

697. Are some people working on multiple Secure coding projects?

698. Does the customer understand the software process?

699. What can you do about it?

700. What are the methods to deal with risks?

701. What things are likely to change?

702. What should be the gestation period for the Secure coding project with this technology?

703. If you can not fix it, how do you do it differently?

704. What is the likelihood?

705. What are the risks involved in appointing external agencies to manage the Secure coding project?

706. How would you suggest monitoring for risk transition indicators?

707. Who are the owners?

708. How solid are the price-volume Secure coding projections?

709. Do you need a risk management plan?

2.35 Risk Data Sheet: Secure coding

710. What will be the consequences if the risk happens?

711. Do effective diagnostic tests exist?

712. How can it happen?

713. Is the data sufficiently specified in terms of the type of failure being analyzed, and its frequency or probability?

714. What are your core values?

715. What are you weak at and therefore need to do better?

716. Has the most cost-effective solution been chosen?

717. What is the chance that it will happen?

718. Are new hazards created?

719. Risk of what?

720. What are you trying to achieve (Objectives)?

721. What are the main opportunities available to you that you should grab while you can?

722. What do you know?

723. During work activities could hazards exist?

724. What are you here for (Mission)?

725. What is the environment within which you operate (social trends, economic, community values, broad based participation, national directions etc.)?

726. Has a sensitivity analysis been carried out?

727. What was measured?

728. What actions can be taken to eliminate or remove risk?

2.36 Procurement Management Plan: Secure coding

729. Are the schedule estimates reasonable given the Secure coding project?

730. Is there general agreement & acceptance of the current status and progress of the Secure coding project?

731. Are there checklists created to determine if all quality processes are followed?

732. Specific - is the objective clear in terms of what, how, when, and where the situation will be changed?

733. How will multiple providers be managed?

734. Are all resource assumptions documented?

735. Are internal Secure coding project status meetings held at reasonable intervals?

736. Are non-critical path items updated and agreed upon with the teams?

737. What is a Secure coding project Management Plan?

738. Are parking lot items captured?

739. Are mitigation strategies identified?

740. Are software metrics formally captured, analyzed and used as a basis for other Secure coding project estimates?

741. Financial capacity; does the seller have, or can the seller reasonably be expected to obtain, the financial resources needed?

2.37 Source Selection Criteria: Secure coding

742. What documentation is needed for a tradeoff decision?

743. How can solicitation Schedules be improved to yield more effective price competition?

744. What is the effect of the debriefing schedule on potential protests?

745. How much past performance information should be requested?

746. Comparison of each offers prices to the estimated prices -are there significant differences?

747. Is experience evaluated?

748. How will you evaluate offerors proposals?

749. What is cost analysis and when should it be performed?

750. What are the guiding principles for developing an evaluation report?

751. Who is entitled to a debriefing?

752. What are the most common types of rating systems?

753. Is the contracting office likely to receive more purchase requests for this item or service during the coming year?

754. What information is to be provided and when should it be provided?

755. In order of importance, which evaluation criteria are the most critical to the determination of your overall rating?

756. How do you facilitate evaluation against published criteria?

757. What can not be disclosed?

758. Have all evaluators been trained?

759. What should a Draft Request for Proposal (DRFP) include?

760. What evidence should be provided regarding proposal evaluations?

2.38 Stakeholder Management Plan: Secure coding

761. Have reserves been created to address risks?

762. What guidelines or procedures currently exist that must be adhered to (eg departmental accounting procedures)?

763. Does the Secure coding project have a Quality Culture?

764. Are cause and effect determined for risks when they occur?

765. Have the key elements of a coherent Secure coding project management strategy been established?

766. What has to be purchased?

767. When would you develop a Secure coding project Execution Plan?

768. Are there ways to reduce the time it takes to get something approved?

769. Are there procedures in place to effectively manage interdependencies with other Secure coding projects / systems?

770. Is there general agreement & acceptance of the current status and progress of the Secure coding

project?

771. Have Secure coding project success criteria been defined?

772. Was the scope definition used in task sequencing?

773. Is the schedule updated on a periodic basis?

774. Has a capability assessment been conducted?

775. Are Secure coding project team members committed fulltime?

776. Is there an on-going process in place to monitor Secure coding project risks?

777. Has a Secure coding project Communications Plan been developed?

778. Alignment to strategic goals & objectives?

2.39 Change Management Plan: Secure coding

779. What is the most cynical response it can receive?

780. What are the essentials of the message?

781. Where do you want to be?

782. Identify the current level of skills and knowledge and behaviours of the group that will be impacted on. What prerequisite knowledge do corresponding groups need?

783. Would you need to tailor a special message for each segment of the audience?

784. What is the most positive interpretation it can receive?

785. What are the responsibilities assigned to each role?

786. What new behaviours are required?

787. Who might be able to help you the most?

788. How does the principle of senders and receivers make the Secure coding project communications effort more complex?

789. Are there any restrictions on who can receive the communications?

790. Has the relevant business unit been notified of installation and support requirements?

791. What risks may occur upfront?

792. Will you need new processes?

793. What are the dependencies?

794. What are the key change management success metrics?

795. What did the people around you say about it?

796. Has this been negotiated with the customer and sponsor?

797. What prerequisite knowledge or training is required?

3.0 Executing Process Group: Secure coding

798. Is the Secure coding project making progress in helping to achieve the set results?

799. Does the Secure coding project team have enough people to execute the Secure coding project plan?

800. How will professionals learn what is expected from them what the deliverables are?

801. When will the Secure coding project be done?

802. How many different communication channels does the Secure coding project team have?

803. What does it mean to take a systems view of a Secure coding project?

804. Does the Secure coding project team have the right skills?

805. What were things that you need to improve?

806. What type of information goes in the quality assurance plan?

807. What is the difference between using brainstorming and the Delphi technique for risk identification?

808. How could you control progress of your Secure coding project?

809. It under budget or over budget?

810. What are the key components of the Secure coding project communications plan?

811. Will outside resources be needed to help?

812. What is the product of your Secure coding project?

813. What are the typical Secure coding project management skills?

814. Have operating capacities been created and/or reinforced in partners?

815. How well did the chosen processes produce the expected results?

816. How can you use Microsoft Secure coding project and Excel to assist in Secure coding project risk management?

3.1 Team Member Status Report: Secure coding

817. How much risk is involved?

818. What specific interest groups do you have in place?

819. Do you have an Enterprise Secure coding project Management Office (EPMO)?

820. Is there evidence that staff is taking a more professional approach toward management of your organizations Secure coding projects?

821. What is to be done?

822. Are the attitudes of staff regarding Secure coding project work improving?

823. How it is to be done?

824. When a teams productivity and success depend on collaboration and the efficient flow of information, what generally fails them?

825. The problem with Reward & Recognition Programs is that the truly deserving people all too often get left out. How can you make it practical?

826. Why is it to be done?

827. How does this product, good, or service meet

the needs of the Secure coding project and your organization as a whole?

828. Does every department have to have a Secure coding project Manager on staff?

829. Are your organizations Secure coding projects more successful over time?

830. How will resource planning be done?

831. Does your organization have the means (staff, money, contract, etc.) to produce or to acquire the product, good, or service?

832. Will the staff do training or is that done by a third party?

833. Are the products of your organizations Secure coding projects meeting customers objectives?

834. Does the product, good, or service already exist within your organization?

835. How can you make it practical?

3.2 Change Request: Secure coding

836. Can static requirements change attributes like the size of the change be used to predict reliability in execution?

837. Are change requests logged and managed?

838. Will the change use memory to the extent that other functions will be not have sufficient memory to operate effectively?

839. How are changes graded and who is responsible for the rating?

840. Who is responsible for the implementation and monitoring of all measures?

841. What is the purpose of change control?

842. Describe how modifications, enhancements, defects and/or deficiencies shall be notified (e.g. Problem Reports, Change Requests etc) and managed. Detail warranty and/or maintenance periods?

843. Who needs to approve change requests?

844. Has your address changed?

845. What must be taken into consideration when introducing change control programs?

846. Why were your requested changes rejected or

not made?

847. What are the requirements for urgent changes?

848. Have all related configuration items been properly updated?

849. How do you get changes (code) out in a timely manner?

850. Will there be a change request form in use?

851. How are changes requested (forms, method of communication)?

852. What is the function of the change control committee?

853. Are there requirements attributes that are strongly related to the occurrence of defects and failures?

854. When do you create a change request?

855. How does your organization control changes before and after software is released to a customer?

3.3 Change Log: Secure coding

856. Is the submitted change a new change or a modification of a previously approved change?

857. When was the request approved?

858. Is the change request open, closed or pending?

859. Will the Secure coding project fail if the change request is not executed?

860. Is the change request within Secure coding project scope?

861. How does this change affect the timeline of the schedule?

862. Where do changes come from?

863. Is this a mandatory replacement?

864. Do the described changes impact on the integrity or security of the system?

865. Does the suggested change request represent a desired enhancement to the products functionality?

866. Is the requested change request a result of changes in other Secure coding project(s)?

867. Who initiated the change request?

868. How does this relate to the standards developed

for specific business processes?

869. Is the change backward compatible without limitations?

870. When was the request submitted?

871. How does this change affect scope?

3.4 Decision Log: Secure coding

872. What is the average size of your matters in an applicable measurement?

873. Is everything working as expected?

874. Do strategies and tactics aimed at less than full control reduce the costs of management or simply shift the cost burden?

875. How do you define success?

876. Who will be given a copy of this document and where will it be kept?

877. At what point in time does loss become unacceptable?

878. Adversarial environment. is your opponent open to a non-traditional workflow, or will it likely challenge anything you do?

879. What alternatives/risks were considered?

880. With whom was the decision shared or considered?

881. What was the rationale for the decision?

882. Meeting purpose; why does this team meet?

883. What eDiscovery problem or issue did your organization set out to fix or make better?

884. What is your overall strategy for quality control / quality assurance procedures?

885. What is the line where eDiscovery ends and document review begins?

886. It becomes critical to track and periodically revisit both operational effectiveness; Are you noticing all that you need to, and are you interpreting what you see effectively?

887. What are the cost implications?

888. How consolidated and comprehensive a story can you tell by capturing currently available incident data in a central location and through a log of key decisions during an incident?

889. How does an increasing emphasis on cost containment influence the strategies and tactics used?

890. What makes you different or better than others companies selling the same thing?

891. Does anything need to be adjusted?

3.5 Quality Audit: Secure coding

892. What does the organizarion look for in a Quality audit?

893. How does your organization know that its staff placements are appropriately effective and constructive in relation to program-related learning outcomes?

894. How does your organization know that its quality of teaching is appropriately effective and constructive?

895. Are adequate and conveniently located toilet facilities available for use by the employees?

896. Do prior clients have a positive opinion of your organization?

897. How does your organization know that the research supervision provided to its staff is appropriately effective and constructive?

898. Is refuse and garbage adequately stored and disposed of with sufficient frequency to prevent contamination?

899. How does your organization know that the quality of its supervisors is appropriately effective and constructive?

900. How does your organization know that its relationships with other relevant organizations are

appropriately effective and constructive?

901. How does your organization know that its system for examining work done is appropriately effective and constructive?

902. How does your organization know that its system for managing intellectual property issues is appropriately effective, constructive and fair?

903. How does your organization know that its support services planning and management systems are appropriately effective and constructive?

904. What data about organizational performance is routinely collected and reported?

905. How does the organization know that its industry and community engagement planning and management systems are appropriately effective and constructive in enabling relationships with key stakeholder groups?

906. Are people allowed to contribute ideas?

907. How does your organization know that its staff support services planning and management systems are appropriately effective and constructive?

908. What are your supplier audits?

909. How does your organization know that its research programs are appropriately effective and constructive?

910. How does your organization know that it is

appropriately effective and constructive in preparing its staff for organizational aspirations?

911. Statements of intent remain exactly that until they are put into effect. The next step is to deploy the already stated intentions. In other words, do the plans happen in reality?

3.6 Team Directory: Secure coding

912. Why is the work necessary?

913. What needs to be communicated?

914. Days from the time the issue is identified?

915. Who are the Team Members?

916. Decisions: is the most suitable form of contract being used?

917. How will the team handle changes?

918. Process decisions: are all start-up, turn over and close out requirements of the contract satisfied?

919. How will you accomplish and manage the objectives?

920. Contract requirements complied with?

921. Does a Secure coding project team directory list all resources assigned to the Secure coding project?

922. Have you decided when to celebrate the Secure coding projects completion date?

923. Process decisions: are there any statutory or regulatory issues relevant to the timely execution of work?

924. Who will report Secure coding project status to

all stakeholders?

925. Who will talk to the customer?

926. How do unidentified risks impact the outcome of the Secure coding project?

927. Process decisions: how well was task order work performed?

928. When will you produce deliverables?

929. Timing: when do the effects of communication take place?

930. Who will be the stakeholders on your next Secure coding project?

3.7 Team Operating Agreement: Secure coding

931. How do you want to be thought of and known within your organization?

932. Resource allocation: how will individual team members account for time and expenses, and how will this be allocated in the team budget?

933. What types of accommodations will be formulated and put in place for sustaining the team?

934. Confidentiality: how will confidential information be handled?

935. Must your members collaborate successfully to complete Secure coding projects?

936. Do you ask participants to close laptops and place mobile devices on silent on the table while the meeting is in progress?

937. Do you determine the meeting length and time of day?

938. What is teaming?

939. Have you set the goals and objectives of the team?

940. How does teaming fit in with overall organizational goals and meet organizational needs?

941. Do you prevent individuals from dominating the meeting?

942. How will your group handle planned absences?

943. What are the current caseload numbers in the unit?

944. What are some potential sources of conflict among team members?

945. Did you draft the meeting agenda?

946. To whom do you deliver your services?

947. Methodologies: how will key team processes be implemented, such as training, research, work deliverable production, review and approval processes, knowledge management, and meeting procedures?

948. Do you record meetings for the already stated unable to attend?

949. Communication protocols: how will the team communicate?

3.8 Team Performance Assessment: Secure coding

950. If you have received criticism from reviewers that your work suffered from method variance, what was the circumstance?

951. To what degree are the goals ambitious?

952. When does the medium matter?

953. Do friends perform better than acquaintances?

954. To what degree can team members meet frequently enough to accomplish the teams ends?

955. To what degree does the teams work approach provide opportunity for members to engage in results-based evaluation?

956. To what degree can the team ensure that all members are individually and jointly accountable for the teams purpose, goals, approach, and work-products?

957. To what degree do members understand and articulate the same purpose without relying on ambiguous abstractions?

958. How do you recognize and praise members for contributions?

959. When a reviewer complains about method

variance, what is the essence of the complaint?

960. What do you think is the most constructive thing that could be done now to resolve considerations and disputes about method variance?

961. How do you encourage members to learn from each other?

962. Is there a particular method of data analysis that you would recommend as a means of demonstrating that method variance is not of great concern for a given dataset?

963. To what degree are the skill areas critical to team performance present?

964. To what degree can team members vigorously define the teams purpose in considerations with others who are not part of the functioning team?

965. If you are worried about method variance before you collect data, what sort of design elements might you include to reduce or eliminate the threat of method variance?

966. What is method variance?

967. To what degree will the team adopt a concrete, clearly understood, and agreed-upon approach that will result in achievement of the teams goals?

968. To what degree are sub-teams possible or necessary?

969. To what degree do team members articulate the

teams work approach?

3.9 Team Member Performance Assessment: Secure coding

970. Are there any safeguards to prevent intentional or unintentional rating errors?

971. What are the staffs preferences for training on technology-based platforms?

972. Are any validation activities performed?

973. What does collaboration look like?

974. What is a significant fact or event?

975. What are the evaluation strategies (e.g., reaction, learning, behavior, results) used. What evaluation results did you have?

976. What steps have you taken to improve performance?

977. Does the rater (supervisor) have the authority or responsibility to tell an employee that the employees performance is unsatisfactory?

978. What are the standards or expectations for success?

979. To what degree will new and supplemental skills be introduced as the need is recognized?

980. How are evaluation results utilized?

981. What are best practices in use for the performance measurement system?

982. Who should attend?

983. To what degree are the teams goals and objectives clear, simple, and measurable?

984. How is the timing of assessments organized (e.g., pre/post-test, single point during training, multiple reassessment during training)?

985. Did training work?

986. Does adaptive training work?

987. How do you use data to inform instruction and improve staff achievement?

988. How is your organizations Strategic Management System tied to performance measurement?

989. How will they be formed?

3.10 Issue Log: Secure coding

990. What are the stakeholders interrelationships?

991. Are they needed?

992. Who were proponents/opponents?

993. Are the Secure coding project issues uniquely identified, including to which product they refer?

994. Do you have members of your team responsible for certain stakeholders?

995. Do you often overlook a key stakeholder or stakeholder group?

996. Is there an important stakeholder who is actively opposed and will not receive messages?

997. Is the issue log kept in a safe place?

998. Can you think of other people who might have concerns or interests?

999. Who have you worked with in past, similar initiatives?

1000. Why do you manage communications?

1001. Is access to the Issue Log controlled?

1002. What would have to change?

1003. What are the typical contents?

1004. Can an impact cause deviation beyond team, stage or Secure coding project tolerances?

1005. What is the status of the issue?

1006. What is the impact on the Business Case?

4.0 Monitoring and Controlling Process Group: Secure coding

1007. How is agile portfolio management done?

1008. What are the goals of the program?

1009. What resources are necessary?

1010. Is the schedule for the set products being met?

1011. How many more potential communications channels were introduced by the discovery of the new stakeholders?

1012. What are the deliverables?

1013. Are the necessary foundations in place to ensure the sustainability of the results of the programme?

1014. Do the products created live up to the necessary quality?

1015. Were escalated issues resolved promptly?

1016. What resources (both financial and non-financial) are available/needed?

1017. In what way has the program come up with innovative measures for problem-solving?

1018. How are you doing?

1019. Did the Secure coding project team have enough people to execute the Secure coding project plan?

1020. What is the expected monetary value of the Secure coding project?

1021. Did it work?

1022. Purpose: toward what end is the evaluation being conducted?

1023. How is agile program management done?

4.1 Project Performance Report: Secure coding

1024. To what degree does the teams work approach provide opportunity for members to engage in open interaction?

1025. To what degree are the tasks requirements reflected in the flow and storage of information?

1026. To what degree is there centralized control of information sharing?

1027. What is the degree to which rules govern information exchange between groups?

1028. To what degree do the structures of the formal organization motivate taskrelevant behavior and facilitate task completion?

1029. To what degree is the information network consistent with the structure of the formal organization?

1030. To what degree are the demands of the task compatible with and converge with the relationships of the informal organization?

1031. How can Secure coding project sustainability be maintained?

1032. What degree are the relative importance and priority of the goals clear to all team members?

1033. To what degree do members articulate the goals beyond the team membership?

1034. To what degree will the team ensure that all members equitably share the work essential to the success of the team?

1035. To what degree do team members agree with the goals, relative importance, and the ways in which achievement will be measured?

1036. To what degree does the teams purpose constitute a broader, deeper aspiration than just accomplishing short-term goals?

1037. To what degree does the teams work approach provide opportunity for members to engage in fact-based problem solving?

1038. To what degree does the informal organization make use of individual resources and meet individual needs?

1039. To what degree do the goals specify concrete team work products?

4.2 Variance Analysis: Secure coding

1040. Did a new competitor enter the market?

1041. What can be the cause of an increase in costs?

1042. Are data elements reconcilable between internal summary reports and reports forwarded to the stakeholders?

1043. Are procedures for variance analysis documented and consistently applied at the control account level and selected WBS and organizational levels at least monthly as a routine task?

1044. Are all cwbs elements specified for external reporting?

1045. What is the budgeted cost for work scheduled?

1046. Are indirect costs charged to the appropriate indirect pools and incurring organization?

1047. Who are responsible for overhead performance control of related costs?

1048. How does the monthly budget compare to the actual experience?

1049. Are all budgets assigned to control accounts?

1050. How do you identify potential or actual overruns and underruns?

1051. What are the actual costs to date?

1052. Other relevant issues of Variance Analysis -selling price or gross margin?

1053. Are meaningful indicators identified for use in measuring the status of cost and schedule performance?

1054. What is the total budget for the Secure coding project (including estimates for authorized and unpriced work)?

1055. How are material, labor, and overhead standards set?

1056. Are records maintained to show how undistributed budgets are controlled?

4.3 Earned Value Status: Secure coding

1057. How much is it going to cost by the finish?

1058. When is it going to finish?

1059. Where are your problem areas?

1060. If earned value management (EVM) is so good in determining the true status of a Secure coding project and Secure coding project its completion, why is it that hardly any one uses it in information systems related Secure coding projects?

1061. How does this compare with other Secure coding projects?

1062. What is the unit of forecast value?

1063. Verification is a process of ensuring that the developed system satisfies the stakeholders agreements and specifications; Are you building the product right? What do you verify?

1064. Where is evidence-based earned value in your organization reported?

1065. Earned value can be used in almost any Secure coding project situation and in almost any Secure coding project environment. it may be used on large Secure coding projects, medium sized Secure coding projects, tiny Secure coding projects (in cut-down form), complex and simple Secure coding projects and in any market sector. some people, of course, know all about earned value, they have used it for years - but perhaps not as effectively as they could have?

1066. Are you hitting your Secure coding projects targets?

1067. Validation is a process of ensuring that the developed system will actually achieve the stakeholders desired outcomes; Are you building the right product? What do you validate?

4.4 Risk Audit: Secure coding

1068. What is the effect of globalisation; is business becoming too complex and can the auditor rely on auditing standards?

1069. Are policies communicated to all affected?

1070. Are all managers or operators of the facility or equipment competent or qualified?

1071. Can assurance be expanded beyond the traditional audit without undermining independence?

1072. Do you have a mechanism for managing change?

1073. What impact does experience with one client have on decisions made for other clients during the risk-assessment process?

1074. Are end-users enthusiastically committed to the Secure coding project and the system/product to be built?

1075. What are the differences and similarities between strategic and operational risks in your organization?

1076. To what extent are auditors effective at linking business risks and management assertions?

1077. Is the process supported by tools?

1078. Do you have an emergency plan?

1079. What effect would a better risk management program have had?

1080. How can the strategy fail/achieved?

1081. Does your auditor understand your business?

1082. Are team members trained in the use of the tools?

1083. Are all financial transactions accurately recorded (receipted, banked)?

1084. What can be measured?

1085. What risk does not having unique identification present?

1086. Does your organization communicate regularly and effectively with its members?

4.5 Contractor Status Report: Secure coding

1087. How is risk transferred?

1088. Describe how often regular updates are made to the proposed solution. Are corresponding regular updates included in the standard maintenance plan?

1089. What was the actual budget or estimated cost for your organizations services?

1090. If applicable; describe your standard schedule for new software version releases. Are new software version releases included in the standard maintenance plan?

1091. What are the minimum and optimal bandwidth requirements for the proposed solution?

1092. What process manages the contracts?

1093. How does the proposed individual meet each requirement?

1094. What is the average response time for answering a support call?

1095. What was the budget or estimated cost for your organizations services?

1096. Are there contractual transfer concerns?

1097. What was the final actual cost?

1098. What was the overall budget or estimated cost?

1099. How long have you been using the services?

1100. Who can list a Secure coding project as organization experience, your organization or a previous employee of your organization?

4.6 Formal Acceptance: Secure coding

1101. Who supplies data?

1102. What lessons were learned about your Secure coding project management methodology?

1103. Was the sponsor/customer satisfied?

1104. What was done right?

1105. Was business value realized?

1106. How well did the team follow the methodology?

1107. Was the client satisfied with the Secure coding project results?

1108. What can you do better next time?

1109. Was the Secure coding project goal achieved?

1110. What function(s) does it fill or meet?

1111. What features, practices, and processes proved to be strengths or weaknesses?

1112. Did the Secure coding project manager and team act in a professional and ethical manner?

1113. Was the Secure coding project work done on time, within budget, and according to specification?

1114. General estimate of the costs and times to

complete the Secure coding project?

1115. Did the Secure coding project achieve its MOV?

1116. Does it do what client said it would?

1117. What is the Acceptance Management Process?

1118. Does it do what Secure coding project team said it would?

1119. Who would use it?

1120. Have all comments been addressed?

5.0 Closing Process Group: Secure coding

1121. What do you need to do?

1122. What business situation is being addressed?

1123. How will staff learn how to use the deliverables?

1124. What is the amount of funding and what Secure coding project phases are funded?

1125. When will the Secure coding project be done?

1126. If action is called for, what form should it take?

1127. What will you do?

1128. Did you do what you said you were going to do?

1129. Can the lesson learned be replicated?

1130. What is the Secure coding project Management Process?

1131. Who are the Secure coding project stakeholders?

1132. Were risks identified and mitigated?

1133. How critical is the Secure coding project success to the success of your organization?

1134. What level of risk does the proposed budget represent to the Secure coding project?

5.1 Procurement Audit: Secure coding

1135. Is there a form specified for bids?

1136. Are there policies regarding special approval for capital expenditures?

1137. Is trend analysis performed on expenditures made by key employees and by vendor?

1138. Has it been determined how large a portion of the procurement portfolio should be managed by the procurement function/unit and how large a portion that should be managed locally?

1139. Are rules in automatic disbursement programs adequate to prevent duplicate payment of invoices?

1140. When tenders were actually rejected because they were abnormally low, were reasons for this decision given and were they sufficiently grounded?

1141. Could the bidders assess the economic risks the successful bidder would be responsible for, thus limiting the inclusion of extra charges for risk?

1142. Is the purchase order form clear and complete so that the vendor understands all terms and conditions?

1143. Are advantages and disadvantages of in-house production, outsourcing and Public Private Partnerships considered?

1144. Must the receipt of goods be approved prior to payment?

1145. Are proper financing arrangements taken?

1146. How are you making the audit trail easy to follow?

1147. Are periodic audits made of disbursement activities?

1148. Is it clear which procurement procedure your organization has opted for?

1149. Does the cash disbursement policy prohibit drawing checks to cash or bearer?

1150. Are information technology resources (e-procurement) used to reduce costs?

1151. Is there a procedure on requesting bids?

1152. Are prices always included on the purchase order?

1153. Are unsuccessful companies informed why tender failed?

1154. Are the responsibilities of the purchasing department clearly defined?

5.2 Contract Close-Out: Secure coding

1155. How is the contracting office notified of the automatic contract close-out?

1156. Change in knowledge?

1157. Was the contract type appropriate?

1158. Parties: who is involved?

1159. How/when used ?

1160. What is capture management?

1161. How does it work?

1162. Parties: Authorized?

1163. Have all contracts been completed?

1164. Have all acceptance criteria been met prior to final payment to contractors?

1165. What happens to the recipient of services?

1166. Was the contract complete without requiring numerous changes and revisions?

1167. Why Outsource?

1168. Change in circumstances?

1169. Have all contract records been included in the

Secure coding project archives?

1170. Are the signers the authorized officials?

1171. Was the contract sufficiently clear so as not to result in numerous disputes and misunderstandings?

1172. Has each contract been audited to verify acceptance and delivery?

1173. Have all contracts been closed?

1174. Change in attitude or behavior?

5.3 Project or Phase Close-Out: Secure coding

1175. Is the lesson based on actual Secure coding project experience rather than on independent research?

1176. How often did each stakeholder need an update?

1177. What advantages do the an individual interview have over a group meeting, and vice-versa?

1178. What was expected from each stakeholder?

1179. Who controlled the resources for the Secure coding project?

1180. What information did each stakeholder need to contribute to the Secure coding projects success?

1181. What was learned?

1182. What could be done to improve the process?

1183. What was the preferred delivery mechanism?

1184. In preparing the Lessons Learned report, should it reflect a consensus viewpoint, or should the report reflect the different individual viewpoints?

1185. What process was planned for managing issues/ risks?

1186. Were cost budgets met?

1187. What were the goals and objectives of the communications strategy for the Secure coding project?

1188. What stakeholder group needs, expectations, and interests are being met by the Secure coding project?

1189. What are the mandatory communication needs for each stakeholder?

1190. What is a Risk?

1191. What were the actual outcomes?

1192. Did the Secure coding project management methodology work?

5.4 Lessons Learned: Secure coding

1193. What is the proportion of in-house and contractor personnel authorized for the Secure coding project?

1194. Who is responsible for each action?

1195. What would you change?

1196. How well did the Secure coding project Manager respond to questions or comments related to the Secure coding project?

1197. What could have been improved?

1198. Were any strategies or activities unsuccessful?

1199. If issue escalation was required, how effectively were issues resolved?

1200. What were the success factors?

1201. What are the internal fiscal constraints?

1202. How comprehensive was integration testing?

1203. What things mattered the most on this Secure coding project?

1204. What were the main sources of frustration in the Secure coding project?

1205. Who has execution authority?

1206. What rewards do the individuals seek?

1207. For the next Secure coding project, how could you improve on the way Secure coding project was conducted?

1208. How well is the build process working?

1209. How effective was the support you received during implementation of the product/service?

1210. What did you do right?

1211. Are lessons learned documented?

1212. How extensive is middle management?

Index

Made in the USA
Las Vegas, NV
22 March 2026

44052711R00175